T0328973

CAMBRIDGE
UNIVERSITY PRESS

University Printing House, Cambridge CB2 8BS, United Kingdom

One Liberty Plaza, 20th Floor, New York, NY 10006, USA

477 Williamstown Road, Port Melbourne, VIC 3207, Australia

314–321, 3rd Floor, Plot 3, Splendor Forum, Jasola District Centre,
New Delhi – 110025, India

79 Anson Road, #06–04/06, Singapore 079906

Cambridge University Press is part of the University of Cambridge.

It furthers the University's mission by disseminating knowledge in the pursuit of
education, learning, and research at the highest international levels of excellence.

www.cambridge.org
Information on this title: www.cambridge.org/9781108813990
DOI: 10.1017/9781108878449

© Sebastián L. Mazzuca and Gerardo L. Munck 2020

First published 2020

A catalogue record for this publication is available from the British Library.

ISBN 978-1-108-81399-0 Paperback
ISSN 2515-5253 (online)
ISSN 2515-5245 (print)

Additional resources for this publication at www.cambridge.org/Mazzuca_Munck

A Middle-Quality Institutional Trap

Democracy and State Capacity in Latin America

Elements in Politics and Society in Latin America

DOI: 10.1017/9781108878449
First published online: December 2020

Sebastián L. Mazzuca
Johns Hopkins University

Gerardo L. Munck
University of Southern California

Author for correspondence: Sebastián L. Mazzuca, smazzuca@jhu.edu

Abstract: Latin America is currently caught in a middle-quality institutional trap, combining flawed democracies and low-to-medium capacity States. Yet, contrary to conventional wisdom, the sequence of development – Latin America has democratized before building capable States – does not explain the region's quandary. States can make democracy, but so too can democracy make States. Thus, the starting point of political developments is less important than whether the State–democracy relationship is a virtuous cycle, triggering causal mechanisms that reinforce each other. However, the State–democracy interaction generates a virtuous cycle only under certain macroconditions. In Latin America, the State–democracy interaction has not generated a virtuous cycle: problems regarding the State prevent full democratization, and problems of democracy prevent the development of state capacity. Moreover, multiple macroconditions provide a foundation for this distinctive pattern of State–democracy interaction. The suboptimal political equilibrium in contemporary Latin America is a robust one.

Keywords: State, state capacity, state building, public administration, patrimonialism, bureaucratization, democracy, democratization, Latin America, Europe, advanced democratic countries

ISBNs: 9781108813990 (PB), 9781108878449 (OC)
ISSNs: 2515-5253 (online), 2515-5245 (print)

Contents

The central political challenge of Latin America in the early twenty-first century is building *high-capacity democracies*, that is, high-quality democracies combined with States that are capable of delivering public goods (e.g., peace, justice, social welfare).[1] Few people would question that the emergence of durable democracies in the 1980s and 1990s is Latin America's most important political achievement since independence. At the same time, however, Latin American democracies exhibit persistent flaws: elections tainted by vote buying and ballot-tampering, candidate intimidation and illegal financing, semi-despotic subnational rulers, and repeated presidential or congressional crises, often resulting in the interruption of elected authorities' terms. No democracy produces a perfect translation of the citizens' preferences into public policies, but Latin America's low-quality democracies create especially large distortions.

Problems of democracy are coupled with problems of the State in Latin America. In general, States do not enforce laws effectively and evenly throughout the country's territory, and in a few cases the very monopoly of violence has broken down. Elected officials frequently use the State as a private or partisan resource, and civil servants owe their positions to political connections rather than merit-based recruitment and promotion. As a consequence, public administrations suffer chronic deficits of human and physical capital, and systematically discriminate against large sections of the population. Millions of Latin American citizens are victims of state failure, manifested in appalling homicide rates, underequipped schools and hospitals, and collapsed transportation and communication infrastructures. Tens of thousands are forced into clientelistic relations in order to obtain, as political favors, a degraded version of the benefits that more capable States deliver as a matter of citizenship rights.

This combination of flawed democracies and low-to-medium capacity States is novel, durable, and understudied. Democracy was never the dominant regime in Latin America prior to the 1990s, and no other region of the developing world has ever combined such a large number of low-quality democracies and dysfunctional States. This configuration is persistent. Latin America has made no progress in building either high-quality democracies or capable States since the 1990s. Indeed, it is caught in a *middle-quality institutional trap*. Yet few studies have addressed how developing societies confront the twin challenges of democratic deepening and capacity building. Thus, this Element poses a key and unexplored question: why, after the great progress of the 1980s and 1990s,

---

[1] We frequently follow the Spanish-language convention of capitalizing the State. We do so mainly as a way to avoid confusion, as could emerge in talking about the state of democracy or the state of the state. However, in phrases that are not open to confusion, such as "state capacity," we do not capitalize the "state."

has Latin American politics stagnated, failing to make further strides toward a high-capacity democracy?

Our argument has two parts. We explain why Latin America's political development has stalled in terms of (1) the interaction between the State and democracy and (2) macroconditions external to the State–democracy interaction. First, Latin American countries are caught in a middle-quality institutional trap because problems of the State suppress causal mechanisms that would foster improvements in the quality of democracy and activate a mechanism that hinders democracy, and problems of democracy block the operation of a key mechanism that could propel the development of state capacity. The State–democracy interaction has not generated a virtuous cycle; rather, it has generated a self-perpetuating equilibrium in which a number of microfoundations sustain the region's middle-quality institutional trap.

Second, Latin American countries are not able to break free from the middle-quality institutional trap because a range of macroscopic factors that affect the State–democracy interaction provide strong macrofoundations. Due to these macroconditions, the political actors who are powerful enough to initiate positive change – either by democratizing the political regime or carrying out reforms to increase state capacity – are opposed to such transformation, and the political actors who would benefit from change lack the power to produce it.

This Element is organized into five sections. Section 1 introduces the research question, considers available answers, and presents the research strategy. Section 2 elaborates a theory of the *mechanisms* that drive the State–democracy interaction and the *paths* countries can follow to become a high-capacity democracy. Section 3 assesses the theory's claim about the paths conducive to a high-capacity democracy by comparing Latin America to Western Europe and some other "advanced" countries over a long time span. Section 4 does the same with regard to the mechanisms that account for the development of a high-capacity democracy. Section 5 addresses the *macroconditions* of the State–democracy interaction in contemporary Latin America. The conclusion recapitulates the key ideas. Finally, the Appendix clarifies the manuscript's key concepts. (There is also an Online Appendix, which discusses the operationalization of concepts and lists the sources underpinning the data and the case studies presented in the text.)

The main aim of this Element is to orient research on the understudied relationship between the State and democracy in contemporary Latin American politics. Thus, we develop a theoretical framework, use this framework to propose substantive arguments, and offer an exploration that opens up avenues for future research. We also present an empirical analysis. However, the goal of this analysis is to ground the theoretical discussion and provide suggestive illustrations of the processes we theorize. Indeed, further refinement of theory and better data are needed before empirical testing is likely to offer conclusive evidence.

1 A Research Agenda and Strategy

1.1 Latin America's Middle-Quality Institutional Trap

Contemporary politics in Latin America is democratic. Indeed, the democratic gains made in Latin America in the 1980s and 1990s are significant and have proved to be durable. Nonetheless, the problems concerning democracy and state capacity are also significant and durable.

Since the 1990s, irregularities involving the manipulation of the electoral process that go beyond the common practice of vote buying have occurred in Bolivia, the Dominican Republic, Honduras, and Nicaragua (Luna and Munck 2022: ch. 5). The competitive nature of elections is affected by the role of money in campaigns. In addition to secret contributions by large firms, resources from corruption have been illegally funneled through kickbacks to candidates in presidential, legislative, and subnational races in many countries, including Argentina, Brazil, Colombia, Mexico, Panama, and Peru (Alconada Mon 2018; Casar and Ugalde 2019; Durand 2019). Criminal syndicates also invest their economic resources to sway election results, supporting candidates who promise political protection (Bailey 2014). Drug cartels have even killed candidates for office and officeholders, especially governors and mayors, in Colombia and Mexico.

The problem of subnational "authoritarian enclaves" is well documented in the cases of Argentina, Brazil, Colombia, Peru, and Mexico (Gibson 2012; Giraudy 2015; Behrend and Whitehead 2016: chs. 4–8; Eaton 2017; Eaton and Prieto 2017). In these instances, undemocratic practices in sparsely populated subnational jurisdictions introduce a distinct bias in the national policy-making arena by turning politicians with dubious democratic credentials into key actors in national coalitions. Moreover, a common pattern is the premature and irregular end of presidential terms in Bolivia, Brazil, Ecuador, Honduras, and Paraguay (Valenzuela 2004; Llanos and Mainstentretredet 2010; Luna and Munck 2022: ch. 5). In Latin American countries that meet the minimal standard of democracy, the right to free and fair elections is not fully guaranteed, undemocratic subnational rulers are overrepresented in national politics, and the prospects of completing constitutionally mandated terms are uncertain. Latin American democracies are largely flawed, low-quality democracies.

Latin America has also experienced many problems of state capacity since the 1990s. The high level of crime – the region has the highest homicide rate in the world (UNODC 2019: 11) – is an indication of the State's failure to monopolize violence. Indeed, some Latin American countries in the early twenty-first century experience "degrees of violence that match those seen in actual war contexts," in part because "nonstate armed actors" have "the capacity to marshal weapons and other coercive means that can parallel if not exceed or undermine those available to the nation-state" (Davis 2017: 66). However, the failure of the State to provide security is not only a matter of relative firepower. Evidence shows complicity between organized crime – big and small – and various levels of the State (Arias and Goldstein 2010; Dewey 2015; Hilgers and Macdonald 2017; Yashar 2018; Auyero and Sobering 2019). That is, the lack of capacity to deal with organized crime is also due to rogue elements within the State that use their position in the State for illegal purposes and prey on citizens in deliberate ways.

Turning from the armed forces to the civil service, studies highlight that Brazil, Costa Rica, Uruguay, and Chile have taken steps to implement merit-based standards for careers in the public administration (Iacoviello and Strazza 2014: 21, 47). However, it is no exaggeration to claim that no country in Latin America has fully developed a rational-legal bureaucracy. Even Brazil, the country held up as an example of state capacity within the region, is best characterized as having only "pockets of efficiency" or "islands of excellence" surrounded by "a sea of traditional clientelistic norms" (Evans 1995: 61; Grindle 2012: 179–84; Bersch, Praça, and Taylor 2017: 164–65). Given the prevalence of corruption (the undue appropriation of public resources for private or partisan gain) and favoritism (the absence of merito-cratic recruitment and promotion) Latin American public administrations are best characterized as patrimonial or semi-patrimonial rather than as bureau-cratic (Mazzuca 2010).

Not all Latin American countries currently suffer from the same combination of political problems. Some countries are more positive than the regional norm (e.g., Uruguay and Costa Rica); others are clearly negative outliers (Cuba and Venezuela). Not all Latin American countries are completely stable since making transitions to democracy. Some have undergone change for the better (Guatemala has made some gains, though maybe fleeting, in the fight against corruption), others for the worse (Nicaragua shows clear signs of democratic erosion). Nonetheless, when viewed from a comparative historical perspective, these differences are better understood as variations within a modal pattern.

The combination of flawed democracies and low-to-medium capacity States is a historical novelty in Latin America. Most immediately, it contrasts with the modal pattern of the 1930–80 period (Touraine 1989; Collier and Collier 1991; Rueschemeyer, Stephens, and Stephens 1992: ch. 5; Garretón et al. 2004).

Moreover, the new configuration has proved to be durable. Many hoped that the transitions from authoritarian rule in the 1980s and 1990s would lead to democracies that deliver what citizens demand. Some observers even claimed that the transitions eliminated any fundamental difference between the politics of Latin America and Western Europe. Yet key differences between Latin America and Western Europe along the two most fundamental axes of political power remain (see Figure 1).[2] Contemporary Latin American politics is caught in a *middle-quality institutional trap*, a stable configuration of flawed democracies and low-to-medium capacity States.[3]

1.2 Building High-Capacity Democracies: What Do We Know?

Why is Latin America currently caught in a middle-quality institutional trap, combining flawed democracies and low-to-medium capacity States since the 1990s? This is a pressing question. Yet we know little about why Latin America has not succeeded in building *high-capacity democracies*, that is, high-quality democracies coupled with a capable State.

---

[2] These data show that Western European countries – or, more precisely, Northwestern European countries – cluster rather tightly in the upper right-hand corner, indicating a high level of both democracy and state capacity, and that Latin American countries, in contrast, are generally not examples of high-level democracy and state capacity. The one obvious exception is Chile. However, the view that Chile in 2008 should be rated as a top performer on a democracy scale is rather dubious in light of the impact of constitutional and electoral arrangements inherited from the Pinochet dictatorship (Garretón 2007: parts 2 and 3). Moreover, analyses of the Pinochet dictatorship, and revelations of various corruption schemes in the post-Pinochet years, raise doubts about how far Chile had gone in breaking with patronage practices (Remmer 1991: ch. 6; Grindle 2012: 172–77, 195–200, 224–26; González-Bustamante et al. 2016). Thus, while the pattern revealed by these data is generally confirmed by other sources of information, some questions might be raised about the placement of specific countries.

[3] This characterization shares some elements with other depictions of contemporary Latin America that stress the problematic nature of politics in the region (Foweraker 2018; Brinks, Levitsky, and Murillo 2019). However, we note some differences as well. Foweraker (2018) holds that current Latin American politics is best characterized as a combination of democracy and oligarchy – which he labels polity – and stresses how oligarchic power is protected by a patrimonial State. We largely share this view. However, though Foweraker (2018: 1, 6) sees the two features he addresses – democracy and oligarchy – as "opposing principles" that give rise to a "contradictory system," we stress the stability of the combination of flawed democracies and low-to-medium capacity States. In turn, Brinks, Levitsky, and Murillo (2019) treat the weakness of institutions, which they define as the failure of formal rules to generate the outcomes sought by their designers, as a key to understanding contemporary Latin America. For example, they see the State's lack of even treatment of the population of a country or the low quality of democracy as a manifestation of institutional weakness (Brinks, Levitsky, and Murillo 2019: 2). In contrast, we see institutions as strong and efficacious when all powerful actors accept them, regardless of their designer's intent, and hence when they are an expression of a political equilibrium. Elections are a prime example of strong institutions in Latin America. Moreover, we do not make any connection between strong institutions and normatively valued institutions, such as democracy and a State capable of providing public goods. Indeed, the middle-quality institutional trap in Latin America is an example of strong, not weak, institutions.

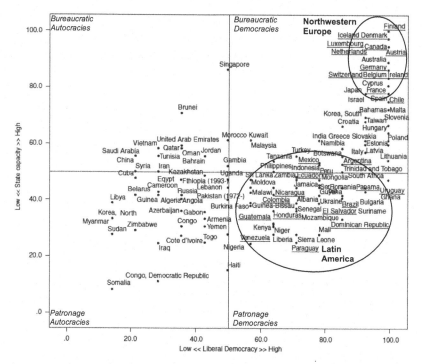

Figure 1 State capacity and democracy: a global perspective, 2008
Note: The data are based on measures of Freedom House's Political Rights and Civil Liberties index, and the Political Risk Service Group's International Country Risk Guide. The thresholds that divide the four cells are due to Pippa Norris.
Source: Norris (2012: 58).

The classic studies on Latin American politics focus on the relationship between economic development and democracy (Germani 1962; Cardoso and Faletto 1969; O'Donnell 1972; Collier 1979; Touraine 1989; Collier and Collier 1991; Rueschemeyer, Stephens, and Stephens 1992). They do not consider the State or do so only in passing. Moreover, when the State is brought into the analysis, it is seen as a second-order force in relation to capitalism and democracy.

Since the 1990s, scholars working on Latin America turned their attention to the State. A growing body of research addresses the State in comparative historical perspective and focuses on various aspects of contemporary state capacity.[4] Thus, in addition to the substantial body of research on the

---

[4] Historical analyses include Centeno (2002), Schneider (2012), Centeno and Ferraro (2013), Kurtz (2013), Paredes (2013), Saylor (2014), Soifer (2015), and Mazzuca (2021). On contemporary state capacity, see Geddes (1994), Huber (1995), Grindle (2012), Arjona (2016), Daly (2016),

capitalism–democracy relationship, we have new knowledge about state formation in nineteenth-century Latin America and about state capacity in contemporary Latin America. However, we have few works that bridge the study of the
State and democracy.[5] The dominant account about Latin American politics
continues to focus on the various political regimes and models of economic
development since independence. How the State fits within the standard
account – and, more pointedly, how democracy and the State affect each
other – remains a surprisingly open question.

In turn, the prevailing account of the State–regime nexus within the broader
field of comparative politics, the State-first thesis, offers a concerning answer to
Latin America's problem. This view, associated with Huntington (1968) and
Fukuyama (2014), posits that the order in which state capacity and democracy
are built makes a big difference.[6] It holds that only one right path to high-capacity
democracy exists: countries build high-capacity democracies by developing state
capacity first and democratizing only after the process of state building has been
essentially completed. The resulting diagnosis of current Latin America is
straightforward: the region's failure to develop much-needed state capacity is
due to the fact that it followed the wrong path, democratizing their regimes in the
1980s and 1990s "prematurely," before building high-capacity States, rather than
following the State-first path.[7]

This highly influential thesis has potentially undemocratic consequences.
Much as during the 1960s and 1970s, when it was argued that dictatorships
were better suited to tackle the challenge of economic development, in the early
twenty-first century the view that democracies are not able to develop state
capacity and may even be a hindrance to capacity building has been broadly
taken for granted both outside and inside Latin America. Drawing on this view,
the idea that the curtailment of democracy may be a cost worth paying to get the
benefits of increased state capacity has gained currency. Indeed, this idea is
more or less directly asserted in many public discussions in Latin America, and
even endorsed by influential voices and organizations.

Yet the State-first thesis has been neither adequately theorized nor empirically validated. As discussed in an earlier work (Mazzuca and Munck 2014), this

---

Dargent, Feldmann, and Luna (2017), Davis (2017), Giraudy and Luna (2017), Lessing (2017),
Yashar (2018), and Bersch (2019).

[5] For exceptions, see O'Donnell (1993, 2001, 2010), López-Alves (2000), Kurtz (2013), Giraudy
(2015), and Foweraker (2018).

[6] Other scholars who are associated with this school of thought are Friedrich (1950: 10–11, 19, 38),
Nordlinger (1968), Rustow (1967), Shefter (1994), Snyder (2000), Zakaria (2003), North, Wallis,
and Weingast (2009), and Wimmer (2013).

[7] The idea of "premature democratization" is commonly used in the State-first literature. See
Wimmer and Schetter (2003), Zakaria (2003: 55–58), Fukuyama (2005: 88), and Mansfield and
Snyder (2007: 7).

line of thinking suffers from a key theoretical flaw. It does not provide a causal argument that accounts for how building a capable State would subsequently generate pressure for a country to democratize rather than simply strengthen the dictator who oversees capacity building. The State-first thesis is a good example of what Falleti and Mahoney (2015: 216–18) call a strictly temporal, as opposed to causal, sequence. That is, it only posits that *when* state capacity is built first a country will ultimately be successful in attaining a high-capacity democracy, but never says *why* this outcome will be achieved.[8] Moreover, the thesis has been rarely tested empirically, and the most relevant tests – comparative historical analyses examining the timing of the development of state capacity and democracy over long periods – raise serious doubts about it (Tilly 2004, 2007; Berman 2019).[9]

In sum, the state of knowledge on how to build high-capacity democracy is thin. Yet, the political challenge faced by Latin America has made the need for answers urgent, and the vacuum of knowledge has been filled by the notion that Latin America democratized "prematurely" in relation to state development and by policy recommendations that make the veiled assumption that state building requires some form of democratization reversal. Before the State-first thesis becomes a dominant ideology, the social sciences must develop theory and analyze a wealth of information about the historical development of States and regimes that has largely been ignored.

---

[8] For example, one of the more carefully argued works that advances the State-first thesis, by Shefter (1994: 14, 36–45), dedicates a lot of attention to the persistence of an autonomous bureaucracy through many regime changes in Prussia/Germany, but never addresses why Germany democratized and does not consider whether the autonomous bureaucracy actually was an obstacle to democracy. That is, although he highlights the importance of "the relative timing of democratization and bureaucratization," he presents a one-sided analysis, offering an elaborate theory of the impact of democracy on bureaucratization but no theory of the impact of bureaucracy on democratization. Moreover, inasmuch as a theory of the impact of bureaucracy on democratization can be gleaned from the works of scholars who support the State-first thesis, it centers on the idea of overload – the relationship between demands and capacity (Rustow 1967: 126, 128; Huntington 1968: 78–92) – and considers only the reduction of costs of democracy to elites (North, Wallis, and Weingast 2009: 25–27, chs. 5 and 6). We consider that this explanation is inadequate, in that the reduction of the costs of democracy to elites determines their resistance to democracy, but offers no account of where demand for democracy would come from. That is, this account would still not be able to explain why bureaucratization leads to democratization.

[9] Several quantitative, largely cross-sectional, studies offer partly relevant evidence, and the results of these tests are decidedly mixed. On the one hand, some studies that claim to support the State-first thesis only show that democracies with more state capacity are better able to deliver public goods, which is not a disputed issue (D'Arcy and Nistotskaya 2017). On the other hand, other studies show that democracies are able to build state capacity and that democratizing before state capacity has been secured does not lead to violence (Norris 2012: ch. 7; Carbone and Memoli 2015).

1.3 Toward a New Theory

Seeking to understand why Latin America is currently caught in a middle-quality institutional trap, we proceed cautiously, in a step-by-step fashion, leveraging the little knowledge available.

We draw on an important insight by Tilly in his pioneering study of the joint development of state capacity and democracy. He argues that it is likely that successful cases of development of high-capacity democracy involve general *internal* processes, but that the *external* processes that shape the State–democracy interaction differ across regions and epochs (Tilly 2007: 22–23, 50, 72–78). In other words, though the mechanisms involved in building high-capacity democracies might be quite general, the macroconditions that shape the State–democracy interaction must be seen as bounded in time and space. Thus, we focus initially on the State–democracy interaction and do not turn to the macrodeterminants of this interaction until we have elaborated and tentatively assessed our theory of the internal dynamics between State and democracy. In other words, we develop an explanation by first looking "inside the box" of the State–democracy interaction and subsequently examining factors "outside the box" (see Figure 2).

We develop the first component of the explanation of Latin America's middle-quality institutional trap by theorizing the causal *mechanisms* that drive the dynamic interaction between state building and regime change, and that make countries either move or stall along a *path* to a high-capacity democracy. We then analyze novel data about the paths followed by countries and the outcomes reached following different paths. We also provide case studies to identify the mechanisms in operation in countries that became and did not become high-capacity democracies.

Here, following in the steps of a rich and productive tradition in the study of Latin American politics, we compare Latin America to advanced countries.[10]

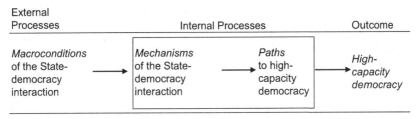

Figure 2 A theory of high-capacity democracy: sketch

---

[10] Kurth (1979), Rueschemeyer, Stephens, and Stephens (1992), Linz and Stepan (1996a), Collier (1999), Grindle (2012), Kurtz (2013: ch. 7), Schneider (2012: ch. 2). See also Centeno and López-Alves (2001) and Centeno (2002).

We do not deny the existence of important differences within Latin America. Indeed, we briefly address some variations across Latin American cases. However, because knowledge about the State–democracy relationship is rather scant, we think that the best strategy is to first understand contemporary Latin America's modal pattern in relation to high-capacity democracies, and to consider variations within Latin America in detail in later research, after some firm knowledge about the region's modal pattern has been established.

Finally, once we draw conclusions about our theory of the State–democracy interaction, we develop the second component of our explanation of Latin America's middle-quality institutional trap by considering *macroconditions*, specific to Latin America, that can sustain or alter the interaction between State and democracy. We consider a range of macroconditions, some political, others economic, some domestic, others international. We analyze whether macroconditions consolidate or could alter the profile of mechanisms in operation in Latin America, either making the region's institutional trap stronger or freeing the region to progress or regress. In this way, we assess the prospects that Latin American countries can break out of their middle-quality institutional trap.[11]

2 The State–Democracy Interaction

As a first step in our explanation of why Latin America is caught in a middle-quality institutional trap and has not succeeded in building high-capacity democracies, we look "inside the box" of the State–democracy interaction and focus squarely on mechanisms. Most processes involve multiple mechanisms, and though some mechanisms drive changes toward a capable State or a high-quality democracy, others do not. Moreover, mechanisms usually work in combination, and the combination of mechanisms determines the path followed by a country and whether this path leads to the outcome of a high-capacity democracy. We develop these general ideas and then relate them to the specific situation of contemporary Latin America.

---

[11] Our full theory identifies multiple actors, their preferences, and outcomes. We also rely on the concept of equilibrium. However, we present our theory verbally, in terms of mechanisms, in line with Tilly's (2007) use of mechanisms. And we conceptualize equilibrium as a property of a system in which no actor that is powerful enough to introduce change prefers change, in line with the notion of equilibrium common in comparative historical analysis (Krasner 1984; Thelen 1999; Capoccia and Kelemen 2007). Thus, we do not offer a formal game theoretic model because game theoretic models with multiple players become mathematically very complicated and might yield no results; because we are considering the existence of multiple equilibria, and the existence of multiple equilibria is largely considered a weakness by advanced game theorists; and because the concept of equilibrium we use does not correspond to the classic concepts of equilibrium in game theory.

2.1 Mechanisms and Mechanism Types

Multiple mechanisms can operate in the State–democracy interaction. This is an insight gleaned from a close reading of works going back to Tocqueville, Hintze, and Weber. However, to turn ideas about mechanisms scattered across a large literature into a theory of the State–democracy interaction,[12] we first systematize these ideas by showing how they are examples of three categories of mechanisms, distinguished according to their source (the State or democracy) and their impact (positive or negative for democracy or the State).[13]

2.1.1 State-Centered Pro-democracy Mechanisms

The first type of mechanism is triggered by state building and has a positive impact on democratization. That is, this kind of mechanism supports the view that initial steps taken to build state capacity can create pressure for subsequent democratization.

One example is the *destruction of social elites opposed to democracy* that is brought about by state building. State building, inasmuch as it involves the concentration of political power in a center that controls the means of coercion and administration, eliminates intermediary powers between the State and the population (e.g., local oligarchies, regional warlords) and destroys some of the key bases of resistance to the creation of universal citizenship, that is, the recognition that each person within a State is entitled to civil and political rights (Bendix 1964: ch. 2, 112–15; Hintze 1975a [1902]: 174–75; Tocqueville 2011 [1856]: 22–27).[14] In brief, the "penetration" of society by the State reduces the power of social actors who defend privileges inconsistent with democracy.

---

[12] We draw on, among others, Tocqueville (2010 [1835 and 1840], 2011 [1856]), Hintze (1975a [1902], 1975b [1906], 1975c [1931]), Weber (1994a [1905], 1994b [1917], 1978 [1922]: ch. 11 and appendix II), Bendix (1964), Rokkan (1970, 1975), Przeworski (1975, 2015), Daalder (2011 [1995]), Laitin (1995), Ertman (1997), Levi (1999), Tilly (2004, 2007), Norris (2012), Raadschelders and Bemelmans-Videc (2015), Acemoglu and Robinson (2016, 2019), and Berman (2019). We also draw on our previous research (Mazzuca 2010; Mazzuca and Munck 2014).

[13] We rely on an explicit definition of causal mechanisms – they are actions of entities at a lower level of organization than the ultimate outcome that is being explained (Coleman 1986: 1322) – and we strive for a representation of mechanisms that is complete, that is, that includes all the mechanisms possibly involved in a process, and internally coherent, that is, that presents a logically organized set of mechanisms (Craver and Darden 2013: chs. 3 and 6; Waldner 2015). Though the idea of type of mechanism and the systematization of mechanism types is acknowledged in the life sciences (Craver and Darden 2013: 67–69), it is practically absent in the social sciences. As far as we know, our theory of mechanisms is the first one to be based on a systematization of types of mechanism in the study of the State and democracy, and even more broadly.

[14] See also Weiner (1971: 177–78), Tilly (1990: ch. 4, 1998, 2007: 76–77, 137–39), O'Donnell (2010: ch. 3), and Acemoglu and Robinson (2016: 25–28).

Another example is the *mass demand for democracy* triggered by state building. State building can stimulate democratization through an increase in the burden the government places on the population (e.g., taxation, military service), which fuels collective demands for the right to participate in the decision-making process (Tilly 1990: 99–103, 115, 1998, 2007: 139–46; Mann 1993: 249–52, 524; Levi 1999).[15] The "no taxation without representation" political maxim (and demand) reflects exactly this mechanism. That is, state building can motivate actors to engage in prodemocratic collective action.

2.1.2 State-Centered Anti-democracy Mechanisms

A second type of mechanism is also triggered by state building but has a negative impact on democratization. Thus, this kind of mechanism highlights a key point: the effect of state building on democracy can be ambivalent. State building can unleash processes that strengthen the social conditions for democracy, while simultaneously unleashing multiple countervailing processes. We identify three such countervailing mechanisms: one involving society, another regime actors, and the last State actors.

One such mechanism is the *destruction of social pluralism*. The process of state building, to the extent that it involves the concentration of political power, can crush autonomous groups in society and intermediary organizations (parties and parliaments based on universal citizenship) that are needed by democracy. That is, the development of state capacity could eliminate the basis for societal pluralism (Tocqueville 2010 [1840]: vol. 4, part 4) and negatively affect a key aspect of the process of democratization – the legitimation of opposition (Rokkan 1970: 28–29, 35–36, 79–83).[16] The State can be a destroyer of societal pluralism and legitimate opposition.

A second example is the *empowerment of dictators* produced by state building. A capable State, with coercive and administrative capacity, can be a formidable obstacle to democracy in that it empowers dictators. If the State has a strong coercive apparatus (Albertus and Menaldo 2012; Bellin 2012) or is able to secure a good economic performance (Haggard and Kaufman 2016: ch. 2), the hand of dictators is strengthened and hence the prospects of democracy are reduced (Acemoglu and Robinson 2016: 29–32). The State can be a source of strength of dictators.

A third example is the *empowerment of State actors opposed to democracy*. State building can give rise to a coercive apparatus or a public administration

---

[15] See also Weiner (1971: 177–78) and Mazzuca and Munck (2014: 1223–24).

[16] See also Hintze (1975c [1931]), Moore (1966: 415–18, 430), Skocpol (1979: part 2), Rueschemeyer, Stephens, and Stephens (1992: 63–69), and Ertman (1997).

that either houses a political class with its own interests or is captured by an antidemocratic social class. Thus, a capable State can be a formidable obstacle to democracy if the State becomes its own master (Gerschenkron 1943: 91–92; Tilly 2006: 23–24, 2007: 184–85) or an instrument of the wealthy against the public. For example, a large standing army, acting on its own interests, or colluding with social actors, can resist efforts at democratization (Hintze 1975b [1906]: 183–84, 187–88, 199–201) or overthrow democracy (Finer 1962). In turn, a well-developed public administration, following its own interests, can work against democratization (Riggs 1963; Weiner 1971: 180) or undermine democracy by usurping decision-making powers, that is, by asserting their power as autonomous actors and substituting their preferences for the commands of elected civilian authorities (Bendix 1964: 159–60; Weber 1978 [1922]: 984–85, 990–94, 1403–10, 1416–19). The State can be a site of resistance to democracy.[17]

2.1.3 Democracy-Centered Pro-State Capacity Mechanisms

Finally, a third type of mechanism is triggered by democratization and has a positive impact on state building. One such mechanism is the *legitimation of the State*. Democratization can be a cause of political order and civil peace because democracy is "a method of processing conflicts" (Przeworski 2010: 24–29, 122–24) that grants legitimacy to the holders of government offices, allows the opposition to hold a reasonable expectation to access power in the future, and thereby induces obedience (Bobbio 1986 [1984]: 53–54, 1989 [1985]: 44–45, 117–24; Przeworski 2015, 2019: ch. 9). Indeed, political exclusion is a source of politically driven violence and the political incorporation of violent groups is a source of pacification (Mazzuca and Robinson 2009). In turn, electoral demobilization rather than electoral mobilization can be a threat to political stability (Przeworski 1975). In brief, democratization is a basis for the legitimacy of the State and is conducive to political order (Norris 2012: ch. 6; Mazzuca and Munck 2014: 1224–26).

---

[17] Taken as a group, these five theses about the impact of state building on democratization diverge considerably from those used in the school of thought that supports the State-first thesis. That school essentially considers that democratization is driven by elite preferences and that democratization occurs when the cost of democracy to elites drops and elites have an incentive to grant democracy. In contrast, the perspective presented here considers multiple actors – societal elites and mass actors, as well as political elites and the government (e.g., dictators, professional politicians, and State agents) – and holds that democratization is never driven solely by a reduction in the costs of democracy to political and social elites, and always involves mass demand, popular contention, and elite resistance (Tilly 2004: 8, 26, 255; Acemoglu and Robinson 2006, 2019).

A second example of this kind of mechanism is the *politicians' incentives for state building*. Politicians who hold elective office, facing the prospects of rotation in government, have an incentive to reform the civil service, since a bureaucratic administration would reduce the costs of losing their incumbency advantage when they are in opposition.[18] Moreover, pressure on politicians to reform the public administration could be exerted by business elites, if they find that the costs of a patrimonial administration outweigh its benefits, and by the mass of voters, if they demand public goods (Polanyi 1944: 14; Marshall 1950: 41–45; Bobbio 1986 [1984]: 27–28). Driven by the ambition to gain access to office, politicians could respond to these pressures by launching state-building reforms.[19]

A key caveat regarding the way democratization triggers pro-state capacity mechanisms must be noted. Democratization is not a hindrance to state building, as argued in the State-first literature.[20] Nonetheless, not all democracies operate in the same way and have the same effect on state building. Low-quality democracies tend to perpetuate problems regarding the State. The distinctive features of low-quality democracies (e.g., electoral clientelism, the influence of money on elections and policy-making, the underrepresentation of citizens, and the premature termination of constitutional terms) mute or prevent the operation of the mechanism through which democracy contributes to administrative reform. Thus, this mechanism operates when democratization goes beyond a transition to a minimal democracy and

---

[18] Silberman's (1993: 66–79) complementary argument suggests various reasons why incumbents might consider bureaucratization a solution to problems of governance.

[19] Relatedly, democratization could be a favorable basis for bureaucratization more generally, for it entails rules that limit the arbitrariness of rulers and treat the governed as equals, thereby creating an antecedent for an impersonal administration based on the neutral application of the legal system to all (Weber 1978 [1922]: 983–91, 567–72). See also O'Donnell (2010: ch. 5).

[20] The State-first literature makes a case for democracy-centered anti-state capacity mechanisms. For example, various authors claim that democratization expands the coalition of actors that make a claim on the State, creating a greater demand by parties to share in the spoils system or patronage, and strengthening actors that block efforts at bureaucratization (Shefter 1994: 14–15, ch. 2; Fukuyama 2014: part 1); and Rustow (1967: 276) argues that a process of democratization that starts before state capacity is built exacerbates tensions among groups that cannot be institutionally contained and leads to "anarchy and civil war" (see also Snyder 2000; and Wimmer 2013: ch. 6). However, these mechanisms do not seem plausible. First, with regard to the public administration, the problem attributed to democracy is not intrinsic to democracy, as research on authoritarian regimes shows that they also rely on patronage (Gandhi 2008). Furthermore, as Laitin (1995: 22) holds, the surge of ethnic conflict that sometimes occurs following the collapse of authoritarianism is "due not to democratization per se but to the weakness of the center amidst the process." Indeed, the data analyzed by Norris (2012: 176) show that, even though States with high capacity are more peaceful than States with low capacity, a transition from a patrimonial dictatorship to a patrimonial democracy (holding state capacity constant) is associated with a reduction in violence. Thus, we do not find these mechanisms to be convincing, and we see this type of mechanism as a rival rather than a supplementary type of mechanism.

involves the removal of the features that make democracies low-quality democracies. In other words, democracy creates an incentive for losers in elections to peacefully accept the result of elections and for democratic rulers to build the state capacity needed to deliver public goods (Tilly 2007: 77; Slater 2008). However, the pro-state reform mechanism linked with administrative capacity will likely lay dormant if democracies are what has been called "clientelistic democracy" (Kitschelt and Wilkinson 2007), "captured democracy" (Acemoglu et al. 2015: 1890–97), and "elite-biased democracy" (Albertus and Menaldo 2018).

2.2 Combinations of Mechanisms

Mechanisms usually work in distinct combinations. Indeed, the importance of considering possible combinations of mechanisms is a key insight of Elster's (2015: 27–34) work, which highlights the frequent operation of "pairs of opposite mechanisms" that counteract each other and hence cancel out their effect. However, mechanisms can interact in various ways, not only blocking change but also driving change, in a positive or a negative direction. Thus, the State–democracy interaction is dependent on the specific combination of mechanisms in operation.

The joint operation of mechanisms exemplifying the two types of positive mechanisms – State-centered prodemocratic mechanisms and democracy-centered pro-state capacity mechanisms – creates a *virtuous cycle*. Gains in state capacity lead to gains in democracy, and gains in democracy lead to gains in state capacity. In turn, the operation of a negative type of mechanism in the absence of any positive type of mechanism creates a *vicious cycle*, whereby State-centered antidemocratic mechanisms reduce the prospects of democracy-centered pro-state capacity mechanisms, and the lack of democracy-centered pro-state capacity mechanisms undermines state building. Finally, the joint operation of mechanisms exemplifying the positive and the negative types of mechanism – State-centered pro- and antidemocratic mechanisms, or democracy-centered pro-state capacity mechanisms and State-centered antidemocratic mechanisms – produces a neutral effect that leads to a *self-perpetuating cycle*. In this scenario, the drive to improve or downgrade democracy and state capacity is cancelled out, and the result is stagnation.

2.3 Paths to High-Capacity Democracy

The operation of different types of mechanism and the way in which they combine determine the path followed by a country and whether the path leads to the outcome of a high-capacity democracy. Indeed, this theory of the causal mechanisms involved in the State–democracy interaction has several implications, some general, others specific to Latin America.

2.3.1 General Implications

First, this theory of the interaction between the State and democracy supports the view that the best path to a high-capacity democracy is the *State and democracy coevolution path* (Mazzuca and Munck 2014: 1224), which corresponds to the broad middle swath in Figure 3. Democratization reaches a limit if it is not accompanied by state building – a capable State is needed to enforce democratic rights – and advances in state building unmatched by advances in democratization can hinder the prospects of democracy (Tilly 2007: 58, 161–65; Mazzuca and Munck 2014: 1236–38). However, when state building triggers pro-democracy mechanisms and democratization elicits pro-state capacity mechanisms, state

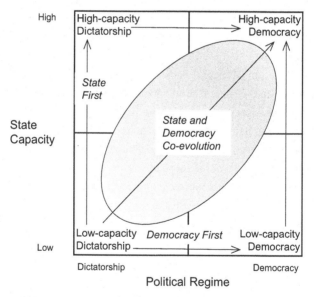

Figure 3 State capacity and democracy: paths to a high-capacity democracy
Note: The arrows in this figure are not meant to indicate that the transition from a low-capacity dictatorship to a high-capacity democracy occurs in two, let alone one step. These paths most likely involve a series of a few big and many small steps. Additionally, though the arrows used to depict paths all end in the strong democracy corner, these arrows are a shorthand to depict some broad successful options. Countries may stall along the way, move sideways, and regress.

building and democratization can advance more or less in tandem, avoiding potential dead-ends.

In the long run, increases in state capacity and democratization reinforce each other. Thus, the key is not what the first step is – that is, whether the initial developments concern state building or democratization – but how the process unfolds, that is, whether the State–democracy interaction takes the form of a virtuous cycle as opposed to a vicious cycle or a self-perpetuating cycle. Indeed, in contrast to the case made by the State-first approach, this theory does not imply the existence of prerequisites for a high-capacity democracy. Given that state building and democratization are never completed in one single step – indeed, they always involve a combination of big and small steps – the key issue is whether the sequence of steps through which state capacity and democracy are built has positive linkages, forming an *integrated sequence* in which one step leads to another.[21]

Second, this theory does not posit the existence of a unique path to a high-capacity democracy. The theory does stress the dangers and difficulties of paths that go to the extreme of either building a capable State without democracy or a democracy without a capable State. On the one hand, building a capable State without democracy can lead to the entrenchment of the dictator who oversees the state building process or to the strengthening of State actors opposed to democracy. On the other hand, building a democracy without a capable State both places a limit on the process of democratization and is likely to lead to frustrations with democracy due to its inability to deliver. However, so long as countries avoid paths that fully ignore either state building or democratization, they can follow a path that, for a considerable period, advances more on the state capacity dimension than the democratic one, or vice versa.

Relatedly, the theory does not assume that paths have deterministic qualities, meaning that once a country starts down a path it will continue to move along the same path. Thus, countries may start on one path and switch their trajectory (e.g., a country may start on a democracy-first trajectory and then begin to take steps combining gains in democracy and state capacity; Tilly 2007: 164–65). That is, the theory implies that one path – the coevolution path – is clearly more likely to lead to a high-capacity democracy than other paths – paths that emphasize the building of only state capacity or only democracy. However, it does not propose a unilinear theory. Countries can build a high-capacity

---

[21] This alternative framing, which places the focus on linkages and linkage effects, is similar to Hirschman's (1958, 1990) "integrated" approach to economic development. For another critique of prerequisites in the context of economic development, see Gerschenkron (1962: ch. 2, 1970: 99–104).

democracy by following *multiple paths*, even *switching paths* and zigzagging their way through a broad middle swath that avoids extreme options.[22]

Third, this theory is not teleological and allows for the possibility that the various paths that are conducive to the creation of a high-capacity democracy will not necessarily achieve the combination of high-quality democracy and a capable State. Countries can *regress* or *stall* in their path. Indeed, the theory acknowledges that the interaction between state capacity and democracy can take one of three forms. When mechanisms combine so as to generate a virtuous cycle, countries make progress toward a high-capacity democracy. When negative mechanisms operate in the absence of counteracting mechanisms, countries regress. When mechanisms combine so as to generate a self-perpetuating cycle, countries stall (see Table 1 for a summary of this theory).

2.3.2 Implications for Latin America

Two implications of this theory are relevant to contemporary Latin America's middle-quality institutional trap. First, this theory suggests that the problem with Latin America is not that it selected the wrong path. Latin America largely fits within the broad middle swath that the theory considers as a viable corridor through which countries can travel on the way to a high-capacity democracy (see Figure 4). Moreover, even though Latin America has made more progress regarding the political regime than state capacity, the flaw is not insurmountable. Countries could switch paths and develop state capacity within the context of democracy.

Second, this theory offers valuable insights about the proximate causes of the Latin America's trap. Latin America finds itself in a peculiar quandary due to the specific combination of types of mechanism in operation. The region has made important strides. Moreover, it has avoided the democratic regressions common in the second half of the twentieth century. But the interaction between State and democracy in the region has failed to generate a virtuous cycle that would move it further along a path to high-capacity democracy. Latin America has stalled along its path to a high-capacity democracy and is caught in a middle-quality institutional trap because the State–democracy dynamic involves a mixed set of mechanisms, positive enough to sustain democratic gains and a modicum of state capacity, but negative enough to block an improvement in democratic quality and state capacity.[23]

---

[22] Again, there is a parallel with the work by Gerschenkron (1962: ch. 1 and Postscript) and Hirschman (1968, 1990), both of whom emphasize the viability of various paths to economic prosperity.

[23] We do not hypothesize which specific mechanisms account for the Latin America's middle-quality institutional trap, and we do not offer any prediction. Indeed, at this time, we seek no more than some orienting ideas to guide empirical research about the State–democracy

Table 1 A theory of high-capacity democracy: mechanisms of the
State–democracy interaction

Type of causal mechanism/causal mechanism	Paths to high-capacity democracy
State-centered pro-democracy mechanisms • State building as the destruction of social elites opposed to democracy • State building as a driver of mass demand for democracy *State-centered anti-democracy mechanisms* • State building as the destruction of social pluralism • State building as the empowerment of dictators • State building as the empowerment of State actors opposed to democracy *Democracy-centered pro-state capacity mechanisms* • Democratization as a basis of legitimation of the State • Democratization as a source of politicians' incentives for state building	*Coevolution.* The coevolution of State and democracy is the best path to a high-capacity democracy. *Multiple paths.* A variety of paths lead to a high-capacity democracy, in addition to the coevolution of State and democracy path; however, extreme State-first and democracy-first paths lead to dead-ends. *Path switching.* Paths are not deterministic (i.e., countries can start on one path and later switch paths). *Path regression and stalling.* Paths are not teleological (i.e., countries on the same path do not all reach the same destination, they can regress or stall).

3 Paths and Outcomes

To ground this theory and evaluate the associated explanation of Latin America's middle-quality institutional trap, we next compare Latin America to Western Europe and some other advanced countries over a long time span (the earliest examples of state building go back to the seventeenth century). Since this group of non-Latin American countries is the only set of cases that has succeeded in building high-capacity democracies, the cross-regional comparison is crucial to

---

interaction, so that the subsequent exploration of macroconditions of this interaction might be able to focus on some previously identified mechanisms. Given the current state of knowledge, this is all that we can ask from a theory.

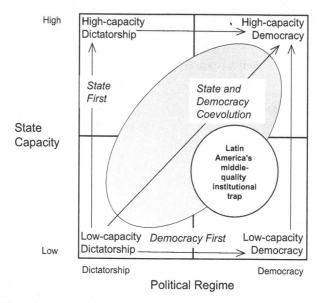

Figure 4 State capacity and democracy: paths to a high-capacity democracy and contemporary Latin America

ascertaining why Latin America, despite having durable democracies, has stalled along the path to high-capacity democracy.

We start by considering the link between the paths followed by countries and the outcomes they reach, and thus shed light on whether the path followed by Latin America explains the middle-quality institutional trap. Since the State's coercive and administrative capacity could be developed at different times, we consider the relationship of democracy to these two dimensions of state capacity separately.

3.1 Measurement and Data

We lack good datasets to assess what paths of political development lead to what political outcomes. We need data that trace developments over a long period, yet most datasets on state capacity and democracy focus on recent times. Additionally, the available historical datasets use only continuous scales and do not measure if and when countries cross the key qualitative threshold distinguishing patrimonial from Weberian states and dictatorships from democracies. Thus, as a first step in an empirical assessment of the theory of State–democracy interaction provided earlier, we generated our own dataset on twenty-one countries (see Tables 2, 3, 4, and 5).[24]

---

[24] The data were coded by the authors based on information in secondary sources. On the operationalization of concepts and a full list of sources used in coding the data, see the Online Appendix.

Table 2 State-and-regime paths and outcomes in Europe and other advanced countries. From the origin of modern states to the 2010s

Country	Creation of modern State: territorial consolidation	State* Coercive capacity: violence monopolization**	Administrative capacity: bureaucratization***	Democracy†	State-and-regime path Sequence order-democracy	Sequence bureaucratization-democracy	Outcome††
Belgium	1830	1830/80s–1940, 1945–2019	1937/39–2019	1894–1940, 1945–2019	State-first	Coevolution	High-capacity democracy
Denmark-Norway /Denmark	1660/1814	1680/90s–1940, 1945–2019	1821/50s–2019	1901–40, 1945–2019	State-first	State-first	High-capacity democracy
Dutch Republic/ Netherlands	1588/1830	1650/90s–1940, 1945–2019	1880s/1918–2019	1897–1939, 1945–2019	State-first	Coevolution	High-capacity democracy
England/United Kingdom	c. 1550/1707	1660/1745–2019	1854/1920s–2019	1867–2019	State-first	Coevolution	High-capacity democracy
France	1532	1660s–1789, 1802–1940, 1944–2019	1790/1900–2019	1848–51, 1869–70, 1875–1940, 1946–2019	State-first	Coevolution	High-capacity democracy
Prussia/Germany	1648/1871	1660/80s–1945, 1949–2019	1770s/1880s–2019	1918–33, 1949–2019	State-first	State-first	High-capacity democracy #
Sweden	1560	1620/80s–2019	1855/75–2019	1911–2019	State-first	State-first	High-capacity democracy
Australia	1901	1947/49–2019	1902/22–2019	1901–2019	Democracy-first	Coevolution	High-capacity democracy

Table 2 (cont.)

Country	State* Creation of modern State: territorial consolidation	Coercive capacity: violence monopolization**	Administrative capacity: bureaucratization***	Democracy†	State-and-regime path Sequence order-democracy	Sequence bureaucratization-democracy	Outcome††
Canada	1867	1871/1910s–2019	1918/20s–2019	1885/98–2019	Coevolution	Coevolution	High-capacity democracy
Japan	1868	1870/80s–1945, 1952–2019	1868/1911–2019	1928–32, 1952–2019	State-first	State-first	High-capacity democracy #
New Zealand	1907	1909/11–2019	1912/20–2019	1907–2019	Coevolution	Democracy-first	High-capacity democracy
United States	1783	1783/85–1861, 1865–2019	1883/1920s–2019	1828–2019	Coevolution	Coevolution	High-capacity democracy

Notes: (*) Dates for coercive and administrative capacity including a slash (/) indicate the period when the core qualitative transformation took place. Dates followed by a dash (–) indicate continuity of the state of affairs. (**) The dates indicate the period when a large standing army was unchallenged. The periods when a standing army is challenged by an organized domestic military force or by the presence of foreign troops are treated as failures of violence monopolization. New Zealand's standing army is best characterized as small. (***) Civil service reform refers to the introduction of exams and merit criteria in hiring and promotion, and other reforms that set up an administration based on the official's commitment to follow legal rules and not to act out of personal loyalty. (†) Dates followed by a dash (–) indicate continuity of the state of affairs. (††) Outcomes followed by a hash sign (#) indicate that the outcome was reached not because but despite following a State-first path, and was largely attained by external imposition. See Table 3 for details.

Sources: Authors' elaboration based on multiple sources, including Mears (1969), Wilson (1999), Childs (2001: ch. 2), and Glete (2002) on military capacity; Finer (1932: part VII), Barker (1944), Rosenberg (1958), Grew (1978), Aylmer (1979), Anderson and Anderson (1967: ch. 5), Mann (1993), Silberman (1993), and Grindle (2012) on administrative capacity; and Bendix (1964: ch. 3), Rokkan (1970: part I), Gerlich (1973), Flora et al. (1983: ch. 3), Rueschemeyer, Stephens, and Stephens (1992), Caramani (2000: 53; 55; 2004: 223), von Beyme (2000), and Przeworski, Asadurian, and Bohlken (2012) on democracy. For a complete list of sources, see the Online Appendix.

Table 3 Democracy in Europe and other advanced countries. From the origin of modern states to the 2010s

Country	Voters: suffrage*			Candidates: competitive elections	Elective offices (elected president and legislature or parliamentary responsibility)**	Period of democracy***
	Non-elite suffrage	Manhood suffrage	Universal suffrage			
Belgium	1894	1919	1948		1831/1857#–2019	1894-1940, 1945–2019
Denmark	1849	1915	1918		1901/20#–2019	1901–40, 1945–2019
Dutch Republic/ Netherlands	1897	1917	1919		1848/1868#–2019	1897–1939, 1945–2019
England/United Kingdom	1867	1918	1928		1688/1834#–2019	1867–2019
France	1824-30	1793, 1848, 1945	1945	Ban on French Communist Party, 1939-44	1792–95, 1848–51, 1871–2019	1848–51, 1869–70, 1875–1940, 1946–2019
Prussia/Germany	1848/71	1848/71	1919–33, 1949	Ban on Social Democratic Party, 1878–90	1918–33, 1949–2019	1918–33, 1949–2019
Sweden	1909	1909	1919		1905/17#–2019	1911–2019
Australia†	1901	1901	1902/67		1901 (1890)–2019	1901–2019
Canada†	1885/98	1920	1920/60		1867 (1850)–2019	1885/98–2019
Japan	1925	1925	1947	Ban on Freedom Party, and Japanese Communist Party, 1894–1925	1887–1945, 1952–2019	1928–32, 1952–2019

Table 3 (cont.)

Country	Voters: suffrage*			Candidates: competitive elections	Elective offices (elected president and legislature or parliamentary responsibility)**	Period of democracy***
	Non-elite suffrage	Manhood suffrage	Universal suffrage			
New Zealand†	1907 (1853)	1907 (1879)	1907 (1893)		1907 (1856)–2019	1907–2019
United States	1828	1856/1924/1965*	1920/1965	Ban on Communist Party of the United States, 1954–2019	1787–2019	1828–2019

Notes: (*) The dates indicate the introduction of a reform to the suffrage. (**) Periods with at least some decisions that restrict parliamentary responsibility are indicated with a hash sign (#). (***) Countries are classified as a democracy based on a minimal definition, that is, elections for top national-level public offices with suffrage extending beyond the elites and without proscriptions of key parties or leaders. In other words, restricted democracies are included as cases of democracy. Many of the cases of interruption of democracy are due to foreign occupation during World War II. By the time all basic restrictions on the right to vote were eliminated, these democracies were all high-quality democracies (even though differences among them persisted). (†) Information in brackets refers to the pre-independence situation.

Sources: Authors' elaboration based on multiple sources, including Rokkan (1970: part I), Gerlich (1973), Grew (1978), Flora (1983: ch. 3), Goldstein (1983), Ersson (1995), Bartolini (2000), Caramani (2000: 53, 55; 2004: 223), von Beyme (2000), Przeworski, Asadurian, and Bohlken (2012), and Bilinski (2018). For a complete list of sources, see the Online Appendix.

Table 4 State-and-regime paths and outcomes in Latin America. From the origin of modern states to the 2010s

| Country | State | | | | State-and-regime path | | |
	Creation of modern State: territorial consolidation	Coercive capacity: violence monopolization*	Administrative capacity: bureaucratization**	Democracy†	Sequence order-democracy	Sequence bureaucratization-democracy	Outcome††
Argentina	Early 1860s	1880–1962, 1963–70, 1980–2019	*1991–92, 2002*	1916–30, 1946–55, 1973–76, 1983–2019	State-first	Coevolution	Middle-quality institutional trap
Brazil	Mid-1840s	Mid-1840s–1932, 1932–2019	*1936–38#, 1967, 1995–97#*	1946–64, 1985–2019	State-first	Coevolution	Middle-quality institutional trap
Chile	Early 1830s	1830s–1891, 1891–2019	*2004, 2016#*	1932–73, 1990–2019	State-first	Coevolution	Middle-quality institutional trap
Colombia	Mid-1840s	Mid-1910s–48, 2010s–2019	*2015#*	1942–49, 1958–2019	Coevolution	Coevolution	Middle-quality institutional trap
Costa Rica	Early 1840s	Early 1840s–1948, 1948–2019	*1954#*	1928–48, 1949–2019	State-first	Democracy-first	Middle-quality institutional trap
Mexico	Early 1850s	1880–1910, 1921–2006	*2003*	2000–2019	State-first	Coevolution	Middle-quality institutional trap
Paraguay	Early 1820s	Early 1820s–65, 1870–1922, 1923–47, 1947–2019	*2008–15*	1989–2019	State-first	Coevolution	Middle-quality institutional trap

Table 4 (cont.)

| Country | State | | | | State-and-regime path | | |
	Creation of modern State: territorial consolidation	Coercive capacity: violence monopolization*	Administrative capacity: bureaucratization**	Democracy†	Sequence order-democracy	Sequence bureaucratization-democracy	Outcome††
Peru	1830s	1840s–1980, 1992–2019	*2014*	1945–48, 1956–62, 1963–68, 1980–92, 1995–2000, 2001–2019	State-first	Coevolution	Middle-quality institutional trap
Uruguay	1828	Mid-1910s–66, 1973–2019	*1943, 1967, 2005–08#*	1919–33, 1943–73, 1985–2019	State-first	Coevolution	Middle-quality institutional trap

Notes: (*) Dates followed by a dash (–) indicate continuity of the state of affairs. The dates indicate the period when a large standing army was unchallenged. The periods when a standing army is challenged by an organized domestic military force or by the presence of foreign troops are treated as failures of violence monopolization. In Costa Rica, the army was abolished in 1949; however, it maintained a monopoly on violence through a police force. (**) Civil service reform refers to the introduction of exams and merit criteria in hiring and promotion, and other reforms that set up an administration based on the official's commitment to follow legal rules and not to act out of personal loyalty. Dates are when a civil service law was regulated. Dates in *italic* indicate reforms that fall short of bringing about a qualitative change from patrimonial to bureaucratic administration. Dates followed by a hash sign (#) indicate that the cumulative impact of reforms is significant, and turn the administration into a semi-patrimonial administration. Dates followed by a dash (–) indicate continuity of the state of affairs. See Table 5 for details. (††) Costa Rica and Uruguay have a semi-patrimonial administration and a high-quality democracy. Brazil, Chile, and Colombia have a semi-patrimonial administration and a low-quality democracy. The other countries have a patrimonial administration and a low-quality democracy.

Sources: Authors' elaboration based on multiple sources, including Centeno (2002: ch. 3) and Mazzuca (2021) on territorial consolidation; Rouquié (1987: part 1) and Loveman (1999) on violence monopolization; Bresser-Pereira (2004), Iacoviello (2006), Longo (2006: 592), Longo and Ramió (2008), Grindle (2012), and Iacoviello and Strazza (2014: 20, 47) on administrative capacity; and Rueschemeyer, Stephens, and Stephens (1992), Drake (2009), Smith and Sells (2017: ch. 1 and appendix 1) and Luna and Munck (2022: chs. 4 and 5) on democracy. For a complete list of sources, see the Online Appendix.

Table 5 Democracy in Latin America. From the origin of modern states to the 2010s

| Country | Voters: Suffrage* | | | Candidates: competitive elections** | Elective offices (elected president and congress)† | Period of democracy†† |
	Non-elite suffrage	Manhood suffrage	Universal suffrage			
Argentina	1912	1912	1951	Ban on CP 1930–38, 1963–64, PJ 1955–73	1862–1930, 1932–43#, 1946–55, 1958–62, 1962–66, 1973–76, 1983–2019	1916–30, 1946–55, 1973–76, 1983–2019
Brazil	1932	1932	1932	Ban on CP 1947–64	1891–1930, 1946–64, 1985–2019	1946–64, 1985–2019
Chile	1925	1925	1949	Boycott of 1927 election by traditional parties; ban on CP 1948–58	1831–91, 1892–1924, 1925–73, 1990–2019	1932–73, 1990–2019
Colombia	1936	1936	1957	Boycott of 1938 election by Conservative party; ban on CP 1954–57; restricted competition during National Front pact 1958–74	1845–1953, 1958–2019	1942–49, 1958–2019
Costa Rica	1885	1913	1949	Ban on CP 1949–75	1848–76#, 1882–1917#, 1920–48#, 1949–2019	1928–48, 1949–2019
Mexico	1857/1917	1857/1917	1954	Ban on CP 1942–78	1855–63, 1867–1913, 1917–2019#	2000–19
Paraguay	1870	1870	1963	Colorado Party is the only legal party during 1937–46, 1948–53; ban on CP 1937–46, 1948–53	1844–69, 1874–1902, 1902–04, 1906–08, 1912–36, 1954–89#, 1993–2019	1993–2019
Peru	1945	1945	1955	Ban on APRA 1932–45; ban on APRA and CP 1948–56	1845–54, 1858–63, 1868–72, 1872–78, 1886–1914, 1915–19, 1919–30, 1931–48, 1950–62, 1963–68, 1980–92, 1995–2000#, 2001–2019	1945–48, 1956–62, 1963–68, 1980–92, 1995–2000, 2001–19

Table 5 (cont.)

Country	Voters: Suffrage*			Candidates: competitive elections**	Elective offices (elected president and congress)†	Period of democracy††
	Non-elite suffrage	Manhood suffrage	Universal suffrage			
Uruguay	1918	1918	1932	Ban on Wilson Ferreira Aldunate and Seregni in 1984 election	1830–43, 1852–53, 1854–55, 1856–64, 1868–75, 1879–83, 1886–98, 1899–1933, 1938–42, 1943–73, 1985–2019	1919–33, 1943–73, 1985–2019

Notes: (*) The dates indicate the introduction of a reform to the suffrage. Though manhood suffrage was recognized in the Mexican constitution of 1857, it was not effectively enacted until 1917. (**) CP = Communist Party. PJ = Peronist Justicialist Party. APRA = American Popular Revolutionary Alliance. (†) Periods with at least some fraudulent elections are indicated with a hash sign (#). (††) Countries are classified as a democracy based on a minimal definition, that is, elections for top national-level public offices with suffrage extending beyond the elites and without proscriptions of key parties or leaders. In other words, restricted democracies are included as cases of democracy. Even when all these criteria have been met, Latin American countries (with the exception of Costa Rica and Uruguay) were low-quality rather than high-quality democracies. Costa Rica was a high-quality democracy since the 1960s, Uruguay since 1989.

Sources: Authors' elaboration based on multiple sources. For a complete list of sources, see the Online Appendix.

The data consist of various measures of the State, the political regime and democracy, the State-and-regime path, and outcomes. Concerning the State, the *creation of modern States* is dated and then the two dimensions of state capacity – coercive and administrative capacity – are measured. With regard to *coercive capacity*, the data registers the periods when modern States secured the monopoly of violence. The formation of a large standing army is the indicator used to mark the initial attainment of violence monopolization. For example, violence monopolization in Prussia/Germany is dated to the 1660s–1680s, the period when a large standing army was formed (Mears 1969: 110–12). In Latin America it corresponds to the formation of permanent armies in the second half of the nineteenth century, as the regional caudillos that emerged after independence were brought under control and military schools were created (Rouquié 1987: ch. 2). Violence monopolization is not always maintained after it is attained. Thus, we also code periods when the State's monopoly of violence was abridged, either due to the territorial occupation by foreign troops, as happened commonly in Europe (e.g., Germany 1945–49), or the presence of domestic challengers, as happened frequently in Latin America when strong guerrilla organizations operated (e.g., Uruguay 1966–73).

With regard to the *administrative capacity*, the data track the bureaucratization of a permanent civil service, that is, the establishment of a civil service in which access to jobs and promotions are based on merit and not on personal or partisan loyalty. Reforms aimed at bureaucratization rarely transform the entire civil service suddenly. Indeed, change is usually introduced in one area or level of the civil service at a time (e.g., ministry by ministry). Thus, we identify the periods when a qualitative change from a patrimonial to a bureaucratic administration takes place. For example, for the United States we use the Pendleton Civil Service Reform Act in 1883, a landmark legislation that initiated the reduction of patronage in the public administration, to mark the start of a process of reform, but we acknowledge that this process continued for several decades and did not result in a full blown bureaucratic public administration until the 1920s (Finer 1932: 1326–38; Grindle 2012: 106–14). Additionally, since no Latin American country has made a transition from a patrimonial to a bureaucratic administration (Grindle 2012: 8, 12, 150–51, 239), we distinguish between countries that had only cosmetic reforms and remained patrimonial administrations (e.g., Mexico 2003) and those that had substantial reforms and became semi-patrimonial administrations (e.g., Brazil, Chile, Colombia, Costa Rica, and Uruguay).

Turning to the measure of regimes and *democracy*, we draw two key distinctions (see Tables 3 and 5). We use a minimal concept of democracy to emphasize the qualitative contrast between dictatorships and democracies. Regimes are democratic when the suffrage is extended to a sizable proportion of non-elites, elections are competitive, and top offices are elected. However, we also differentiate the degree of democracy by distinguishing high-quality democracies from low-quality democracies in terms of the greater extension of the right to vote and the effective guarantee of voting rights, the more competitive nature of elections and the effective guarantee of the right to run for office, the greater proportionality of the translation of votes to seats, and the greater respect for constitutional terms and non-interference in government decision-making by unelected actors. This second distinction is critical because it serves to differentiate Latin American countries from European and other advanced countries in the contemporary period. As noted earlier, most Latin American democracies are low-quality democracies. In contrast, though European and other advanced countries have had low-quality democracies in their early development, since World War II their democracies have been – with only a few exceptions – high-quality democracies.

Finally, the concepts of *State-and-regime path* and *outcomes* are measured by combining the data on the State and democracy. We distinguish between three State-and-regime paths: State-first, democracy-first, and the coevolution of State and democracy. And we code cases in light of the timing of developments regarding the State and democracy. For example, Denmark is a clear case of a State-first sequence leading to a high-capacity democracy, in that it fully developed both coercive and administrative capacity long before it started a process of democratization. In turn, Colombia is a clear case of the coevolution of State and democracy leading to middle-quality institutions, in that it built both coercive and administrative capacity through a process that overlapped, at least in part, with the process of democratization, and has developed a semi-patrimonial administration and a low-quality democracy.

3.2 Coercive Capacity and Democracy

To analyze the pattern in these data, we focus first on the development of coercive state capacity and democracy, and then on the development of administrative state capacity and democracy, considering patterns in Western European and other advanced countries first and then turning to Latin America. Moreover, to better grasp broad patterns, we rely on a simplified graphic representation of the data that highlights broad trends (e.g., it abstracts from temporary reversals, as occurred with the monopoly of violence during the 1789 revolution in France).

The trajectories followed by Western European and other advanced countries in the development of coercive state capacity and democracy can be summarized as follows (see Figure 5, panel a). Overall, most of the countries that were successful in building sustainable high-capacity democracies developed coercive

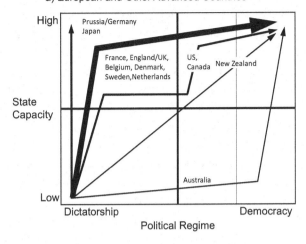

a) European and Other Advanced Countries

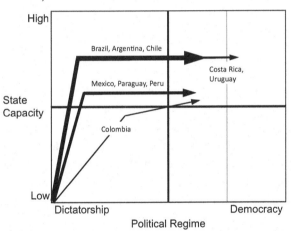

b) Latin America

Figure 5 State-and-regime paths and outcomes. Coercive capacity and democracy in advanced and Latin American countries

Note: The lines in these figures present a summary of the trajectories followed by each country, since their earliest developments (the 1620s in Europe and the 1820s in Latin America) to the 2010s. They offer a simplified view, that does not convey each twist and turn in a country's history and, importantly, some regressions away from state capacity and democracy. The thickness of the lines is proportional to the number of cases that follow a given trajectory.

Sources: The underlying data are presented in Tables 2, 3, 4, and 5. The operationalization of the concepts of coercive state capacity, democracy, and state-and-regime paths; and the sources used in generating the data are presented in the Online Appendix.

capacity, through the creation of large standing armies, before they democratized. That is, a capable State was built before democracy. Nonetheless, this is not the entire story. In New Zealand, the United States, and Canada, coercive state capacity and democracy co-evolved; and in Australia, democracy was in place before steps were taken to set up a standing army. Moreover, in some cases that followed the State-first path (Prussia/Germany, Japan), the empowerment of the State undermined the prospects of democracy and the construction of a high-capacity democracy stalled. Though Prussia/Germany and Japan eventually became high-capacity democracies, it was due to foreign imposition following military defeat and not due to endogenous developments. Thus, advanced countries followed multiple paths to a high-capacity democracy, and the most extreme cases of State-first trajectory led to a dead-end.

In Latin America, most countries followed a moderate State-first path, building large standing armies that maintained order before democratizing (see Figure 5, panel b).[25] However, adding nuance to the graphic depiction of trajectories, it is worth noting that several countries experienced regressions throughout the twentieth century and that, in several cases, losses of democracy coincided with losses in state capacity. Thus, in Colombia, the exclusionary nature of politics in the post–World War II years encouraged the rise of challenges to the State's monopoly of the use of violence. In turn, the way in which state capacity was restored in tandem with democratization highlights that many Latin American countries followed a coevolution path. In Argentina, Brazil, and Uruguay, order was restored under dictatorships in the 1970s prior to democratization. Yet, Colombia re-monopolized violence in the 2010s under democracy and through reforms aimed at incorporating former guerrillas into the electoral process; and, to bring in the experience of countries not included in our data, order and democracy were built simultaneously in El Salvador, Guatemala, and Nicaragua in the 1980s–1990s.

Thus, the big difference between Latin American and advanced countries is not the path they followed but rather that Latin American countries have not reached the same outcome as advanced countries. Latin American countries have stalled in their path, currently having some States that are unable to control violence within their territory and democracies that display many flaws that are closely associated with the State's lack of coercive capacity.

3.3 Administrative Capacity and Democracy

The trajectories related to the development of administrative state capacity and democracy followed by Western European and other advanced countries reveal

---

[25] In three nineteenth-century cases (Mexico, Colombia, and Uruguay), proto-democratic partisan competition preceded violence monopolization by decades.

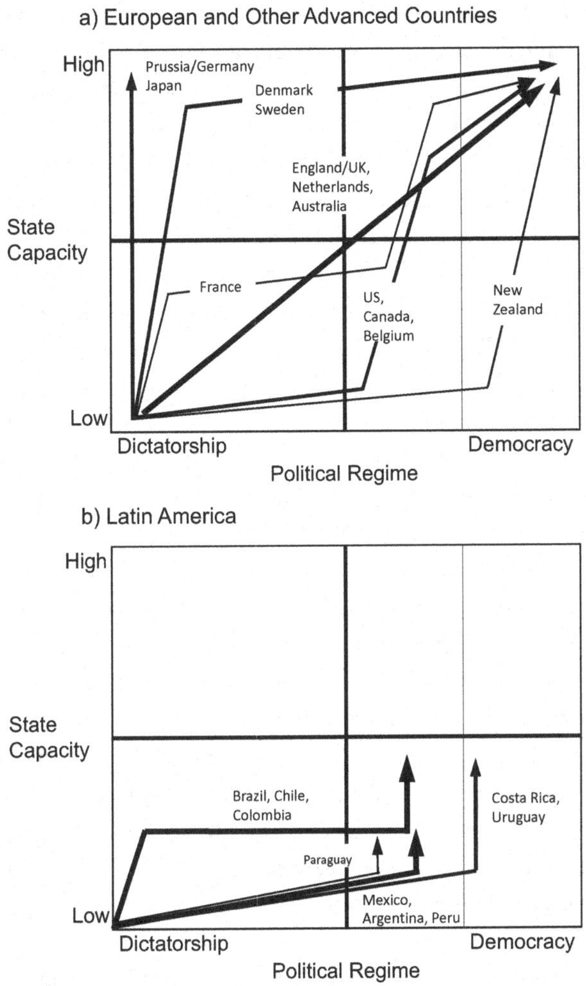

Figure 6 State-and-regime paths and outcomes. Administrative capacity and democracy in advanced and Latin American countries

Note: The lines in these figures present a summary of the trajectories followed by each country, since their earliest developments (the 1620s in Europe and the 1820s in Latin America) to the 2010s. They offer a simplified view, that does not convey each twist and turn in a country's history and, importantly, some regressions away from state capacity and democracy. The thickness of the lines is proportional to the number of cases that follow a given trajectory.

Sources: The underlying data are presented in Tables 2, 3, 4, and 5. The operationalization of the concepts of administrative state capacity, democracy, and State-and-regime paths; and the sources used in generating the data are presented in the Online Appendix.

a pattern that is even more unexpected from the perspective of the State-first thesis (see Figure 6, panel a). The early bureaucratization of the public administration led to the later building of a high-capacity democracy in only two cases (Denmark, Sweden); in the most extreme cases of a State-first trajectory (Prussia/Germany, Japan), the capable civil service developed under dictatorship became an obstacle to democratization and the endurance of democracy. In fact, most of the successful cases, which reached the outcome of a democracy combined with a bureaucratic administration, followed alternative paths. Bureaucratization was implemented either jointly with democratization (France, UK, Netherlands, Australia, US, Canada, Belgium) or after the process of democratization had been substantially completed (New Zealand). Thus, the record shows that countries have succeeded in building high-capacity democracies by following a wide range of paths and rarely by building state capacity under dictatorship. Indeed, the administrative capacity–democracy trajectories offer more examples of countries that followed a path in which gains in state capacity were tightly linked with gains in democracy – in a lockstep process – than is the case regarding the coercive capacity–democracy trajectories.[26]

Turning to the trajectories followed by Latin American countries (Figure 6, panel b), the paths followed by Latin American countries do not vary considerably and can be quickly summarized. Early in their histories, countries carried out partial or little reform of the public administration. Later, in the post–World War II period, but especially in the 1980s and 1990s, regimes were more or less fully democratized. Finally, more or less ambitious reforms that fall short of bureaucratization – the distinction between patrimonial and semi-patrimonial administrations captures a key difference within Latin America – were carried out under democracy.

However, to better appreciate the distinctiveness of Latin America's political development, two key points should be underscored. First, the record of state reform under dictatorship in Latin America has been meager. State building under dictatorship has been rare and the progress made through such attempts has been partial at best. Typical cases are the nearly century-long dictatorship in Mexico (Grindle 2012: 169–72, 189–95, 220–24) and the brutal dictatorships in South and Central America during the 1970s and 1980s (e.g., Argentina 1976–83, Chile 1973–90, and Guatemala 1970–86), none of which built a capable State. Indeed, even in cases such as Argentina, with its frequent dictatorships, "[m]ilitary regimes used patronage to recolonize the public

---

[26] As Møller (2015) shows, the case for the early development of democracy relative to state capacity is even stronger if medieval representative institutions, though certainly not democratic according to the criteria used here, are treated as proto-democratic or precursors of democracy.

administration" and hence dictators were not agents of state building (Grindle 2012: 168).

Furthermore, in dictatorships that have a reputation for reforming their public administration, these reforms were limited or even nonexistent. Most significantly, Brazil stands out as a country that took important steps to develop state capacity before democratizing, under President Vargas in 1936–38 (Touraine 1989: ch. 1; Grindle 2012: 15, 178). Yet Brazil did not succeed in eradicating patrimonialism under dictatorship.[27] In turn, the Pinochet-led dictatorship in Chile (1973–90) is sometimes cited as an example of state strengthening. However, the Pinochet government continued the patronage politics of the previous period (Grindle 2012: 174) and caused a deterioration of the civil service (González-Bustamante et al. 2016: 63; González-Bustamante 2018: 778). Thus, a comparison of the record of dictatorships and democracies in Latin America shows that the failure to build state capacity is not distinctive of democracies. Dictatorships in Latin America have not succeeded in transforming patrimonial administrations into bureaucratic administrations. Moreover, the progress made in building state capacity under democracy has been at least as large as under dictatorship.

Second, the main difference with regard to the development of administrative state capacity and democracy in Latin America and advanced countries is not the path followed by Latin American countries. Indeed, Latin America does not diverge fundamentally from advanced countries in terms of the path followed. However, there is a stark difference between Latin America and the advanced countries in terms of the distance traveled down each path. No Latin American country ever carried out a qualitative transformation of its public administrations and most became only low-quality democracies.

3.4 Conclusions

Contemporary Latin America is not caught in a middle-quality institutional trap because it failed to pursue the path followed by European and other successful countries and opted instead for the wrong path. It is not the case that Latin America democratized "prematurely" before building state capacity.

The notion that a European model exists and that the key to achieve high-capacity democracy is to follow the State-first path is deeply entrenched in conventional wisdom and policy circles (Rose and Shin 2001: 334; King and

---

[27] Graham (1968: 6–7) highlights the "considerable discrepancy between [legal] norms and reality" and argues that, despite the Vargas reforms, "the continuance of a functioning patronage system" during the 1945–64 period was apparent (see also Grindle 2012: 179–84, 204–08). Moreover, reforms under the 1964–85 dictatorship did not fundamentally change the system (Grindle 2012: 208–09; Hagopian 1994, 1996).

Lieberman 2009: 570; Fukuyama 2011: 459; Stillman 2015). Yet, it is simply wrong. First, no single European model exists – let alone an advanced country model. Rather, the experience of European and other advanced countries is varied: they have built stable high-capacity democracies by following multiple paths.[28] Especially as concerns the development of administrative capacity and democracy, most countries have become high-capacity democracies by following the coevolution of State and democracy path. Second, the State-first path has in several cases led to a distinct dead-end, that is, the construction of a capable State and a stable dictatorship, and in those cases high-capacity democracies were only attained after a major exogenous shock, such as a military defeat followed by foreign intervention.

Latin America has been less successful than Western European and other advanced countries. The monopoly of violence is currently challenged in many countries. Despite some success at reforming the public administration, no country has built a bureaucratic administration. Although significant advances in democratizing regimes have been made, most countries have low-quality democracies. That is, Latin American countries have not built high-capacity democracies.

However, this outcome is not due to the path followed by Latin American countries. Successful countries built high-capacity democracies by following similar paths. Moreover, inasmuch as Latin America has made more progress at democratizing than building state capacity, the record of Latin America itself does not indicate that its greater progress on the democracy front is a hindrance to its political development. After all, some advanced countries made great strides in democratizing before developing state capacity, and the historical record shows that Latin American democracies have performed as well or better than dictatorships in building state capacity.

4 Mechanisms and Outcomes

The fact that Latin America has been less successful than Western European and other advanced countries despite following similar paths is puzzling. Thus, in what follows we probe deeper, guided by our theory of the State–democracy interaction, in search of the mechanisms that might account for the contrast between cases that were successful in making a transition to a high-capacity democracy and cases that exemplify the middle-quality institutional trap in contemporary Latin America.

---

[28] For studies that arrive at the same conclusion, see Weber (1978 [1922]: 984), Daalder (1966: 60–61, 2011 [1995]: 42–47), Grew (1978: 2), Mann (1993: 466–67, 469), Tilly (2004, 2007), and Berman (2019: 394, 396). See also Croissant and Hellmann (2020) and Vu (2020).

To this end, we first offer brief discussions of France, England/UK, and the United States. The purpose of these mini-case studies is to have a real-world benchmark for the Latin American cases. Then, a longer discussion of contemporary Brazil, Mexico, and Argentina shows that Latin America has stalled in its path and not made a transition to high-capacity democracy because the combination of mechanisms is different from the one in the advanced countries.

4.1 Advanced Countries

4.1.1 France

The 1789 revolution radically altered France's path of development. France had taken important steps toward the achievement of the monopoly of violence under the old absolutist regime (Bien and Grew 1978: 236–40; Finer 1997b: 1308–35; Tilly 2004: ch. 5). However, it only began to reform the public administration in the wake of the 1789 revolution (e.g., abolishing the sale of public offices), taking further steps toward bureaucratization under democratic regimes, first in 1848–51 and then after 1875 (Finer 1932: 1316–26; Aylmer 1979: 180–81; Grindle 2012: 87–91). State building never got too far ahead of democratization, and vice versa, especially after 1848. Thus, it was only through the changes brought about after 1789 that France developed a high level of state capacity (Tilly 1989, 1990: 107–14, 2004: ch. 4). The main drawback of the path followed by France was political instability: its democracy was fragile, breaking down in 1851, 1870, and 1940. However, France shows that a high-capacity democracy can be achieved by following a State-first path in violence monopolization and a coevolution path in democratization and bureaucratization.

A distinct set of mechanisms was activated in France. The initial process of state building, under the old absolutist regime, established a basis for citizenship more clearly than in other cases by centralizing power and eroding the basis of political power of regional aristocrats. State building undermined the social elites who resisted democracy so as to defend their feudal privileges. However, the process of state building was not completed under absolutism (Rueschemeyer, Stephens, and Stephens 1992: 87–88). Crucial to building state capacity was a reinforcing dynamic between State and democracy.

On the one hand, state building triggered mass demand for democracy, which fueled the 1789 revolution that dislodged the old absolutist rulers (Hoffman 1994; Markoff 1996). On the other hand, democracy fostered state building. Democracy legitimated rulers and brought an end to regime-related violence, the last major incident being the Paris Commune of 1871 (Tilly 1993: ch. 5). Democracy also created an incentive for politicians to bureaucratize the State. Starting in 1789 and gaining new force after 1848, the political movement for legal equality spread from the regime to the State. Indeed, the onset of reforms to end venality was a direct outcome of the French revolution (Finer 1932: 1240–50), and open competitive entrance examinations were introduced by stages between 1875 and 1900, that is, along with democratization (Aylmer 1979: 180–81; Bezes and Lodge 2011). The 1789 revolution placed France on a path of coevolution, and the French case shows how democratization and state building can be mutually reinforcing processes.

4.1.2 Great Britain

Great Britain developed coercive capacity relatively early. By the time Great Britain began to democratize, in the mid-nineteenth century, it had already achieved violence monopolization, which can be traced to the mid-eighteenth century (Brewer 1990; Braddick 2000: part III; Tilly 2004: 134–38). Nonetheless, Great Britain also exemplifies how state building and democratization may coevolve. Key reforms of the civil administration were introduced in the 1850s–1870s, precisely at the time when the suffrage expanded, and thereafter democratization and bureaucratization advanced in tandem. Great Britain's political development is similar to France's, with the important distinction that Great Britain's democratization was a more gradual but also more limited process–e.g., the continued power of the unelected House of Lords through 1911 (Richards 1963; Garrard 2002; Ziblatt 2017: chs. 3–5). Thus, Great Britain is a State-first case with regard to the development of coercive capacity, but a rather pure case of coevolution of administrative capacity and democracy.

The mechanisms in operation during Great Britain's transition to high-capacity democracy are key. First, one of the drivers of democratization was the expansion of the State's role in the wake of the Industrial Revolution, which, through the rise of the urban working class, translated into a mass demand for democracy (Polanyi 1944: chs. 7, 12, and 14; Rueschemeyer, Stephens, and Stephens 1992: 95–97; Mann 1993: ch. 4; Collier 1999: 61–66).[29] Second, democratization fostered state capacity in two ways. The democratic legitimation of rulers largely ended violent disputes over access to top offices; indeed, the violence in Ireland in the twentieth century was more nationalist- than regime-driven (Tilly 1993: ch. 4). Additionally, democratization created an incentive for politicians to bureaucratize the administration, as the following sequence of events shows.

The issue of civil service reform was initially raised with the 1854 Northcote–Trevelyan Report, precisely at the time when reforms to expand the suffrage

---

[29] The same mechanism was in operation in earlier periods, when gains in representation were made (Tilly 1990: 64, 102–03; Mann 1986: ch. 14).

were under consideration. Then, most critically, the expansion of the suffrage in 1867, which extended voting rights to workers for the first time and could be considered the starting point of the process of democratization (Collier 1999: 61–62; Saunders 2011), played a role in breaking the opposition to civil service reform. It was the prospect of alternation in office, which would be decided by an electorate including workers, that led conservative political leaders to adopt reforms that did much to eliminate patronage in the civil administration and to introduce competitive exams as the criteria for staffing the administration (Finer 1932: 1281–303; Shefter 1994: 11, 47–48; Grindle 2012: 81–87).

The path followed by Great Britain was smoother than the one followed by France. However, it further shows how state building provides an impetus to democratization and democratization, in turn, provides an impetus to state building.

4.1.3 United States

The United States is a case in which a high-capacity democracy was built through intertwined developments affecting the State and democracy. The United States started out by developing coercive capacity and soon initiated a process of democratization. This development was interrupted and set back during the 1861–65 civil war, in which a crisis of democracy led to a challenge to the State's monopoly of violence. Yet, thereafter, during Reconstruction, the processes of democratization was resumed jointly with the reestablishment of political order. The development of administrative capacity and democracy also evolved in tandem. Indeed, the bureaucratization of the civil service was launched with the Pendleton Civil Service Reform Act in 1883, in the recently reestablished democracy (Finer 1932: 1326–38). The United States is an even clearer case of coevolution of state capacity and democracy than France and Great Britain, in that the developments of the two dimensions of state capacity – coercive and administrative capacity – and of democracy were interconnected, and developments concerning state capacity and democracy never outpaced the other by much.

Several mechanisms underpin this path. A first mechanism is the mass demand for democracy triggered by the process of state building. The slogan "no taxation without representation" expressed a grievance of American colonists against British rule, and also gave impetus to a process of democratization in the early years of the new country (Wood 1969: chs. 5 and 15; Mann 1993: ch. 5). However, the path to a high-capacity democracy in the United States was hampered by a lack of state capacity.

Due to the compromise that preserved slavery in parts of the country in the early years of the United States – a compromise first enshrined in the 1787 constitution and then in the 1820 Missouri Compromise (Dahl 2003: 13, 15–16; Weingast 1998) – antidemocratic regional elites not only survived but also became key players. First, the slave-owning oligarchies blocked democratization. Indeed, democratization had a limit because the compromise on the issue of slavery placed a racial boundary on the principle of universal citizenship. Second, when electoral results challenged the economic interests of the slave-owning oligarchies, they eventually defied the State's monopoly of violence. That is, state weakness limited democratization, and problems of democracy led to an ever more serious challenge to the State's capacity, the civil war of 1861–65.

A big step forward was thus taken as a result of the outcome of the civil war, which concentrated power in the federal government and, by destroying elite resistance to democracy in the South, gave a renewed impulse to the process of democratization (Moore 1966: ch. 3). The growing democratic legitimation of the State, in part due to the political incorporation of the states of the former Confederacy, counteracted possible challenges to the State's monopoly of violence. But the post–civil war weakening of the regional basis of political power of Southern slavocrats did not eliminate their ability to resist universal citizenship in their Southern bastions. Indeed, the path followed by the United States involved regression, in the aftermath of Reconstruction, and was long; democracy remained racially restricted for nearly a century, until a further use of power by the federal government removed a lingering obstacle to democratization in the mid-1960s (Rueschemeyer, Stephens, and Stephens 1992: 126–32; Mickey 2015). However, the dynamic interaction between State and democracy after the civil war eventually pushed the United States on a path toward greater democracy and coercive state capacity.

A different mechanism was at play concerning the civil service, which was notorious for its patrimonialism from the 1830s to the 1870s. As the costs of politically driven appointments to the civil administration grew and as both public opinion and business interests started to support reform, a key reform bill – the Pendleton Civil Service Reform Act – was passed by Congress in 1883. Thereafter, the reform process unfolded over a period of several decades, through the 1920s, under democracy. That is, bureaucratization occurred under democracy or, more precisely, when the United States was democratizing, as mass demand for, and elite interest in, administrative reform grew and created an incentive for politicians to reform the administration (Finer 1932: 1326–38; Skowronek 1982: 47–84, ch. 6; Shefter 1994: ch. 3; Grindle 2012: 60–66, 91–96, 106–14).

In short, the case of the United States shows that state building and democratization can be mutually reinforcing processes, with the interesting twist that in the United States the coevolution of State and democracy applies both to the development of coercive and administrative capacity. Furthermore, the case adds weight to the point that countries that succeed in building high-capacity democracies did so because the combination of pro-democracy and pro-state capacity mechanisms kept them moving on a path toward a high-capacity democracy (see Table 6).

4.2 Latin America

4.2.1 Brazil

The political dynamic in contemporary Latin America has been different. Brazil democratized in the 1980s and started its current democratic period with a relatively high degree of coercive capacity but only modest administrative capacity – prior reforms had introduced what could be called a semi-patrimonial administration (Grindle 2012: 162–66, 178–84, 205–10). However, following democratization in the 1980s, Brazil has made few strides toward a high-capacity democracy.

Brazil's post-1985 democracy has three advantages over its 1946–64 democracy. Democracy is durable, suffrage universal, and alternation in office frequent. However, a syndrome of informal political institutions make Brazil's democracy a low-quality one. Elections are rife with clientelism. Representation is weakened by the pervasive role of large-scale corruption. Lawmaking is routinely based on the exchange of particularistic favors, if not the purchase of legislators' votes. Furthermore, the impeachment of Rousseff in 2016 and the electoral proscription of Lula in 2018 reveal serious challenges to the right to complete constitutionally mandated terms and to run for office (Kingstone and Power 2017).

With regard to public administration, Brazil enacted a civil service reform in 1995–97, which produced advances. However, it did not eradicate patrimonialism and eventually the reform's momentum waned (Grindle 2012: 210–15; Nunberg and Pacheco 2016; Cavalcante and Carvalho 2017). Indeed, Brazil has a partially reformed public administration, where corruption scandals are recurrent, and recruitment is based on private or partisan considerations rather than on legal, merit-based criteria. Thus, the important democratic gains made by Brazil in the 1980s have not been followed by further progress toward a high-capacity democracy. Rather, Brazil has stalled politically and has not shown signs of moving out of its middle-quality institutional trap.

The mechanisms in operation, as expected, differ from those found in France, Britain, and the United States. On the one hand, democratization has had a mixed impact. The democratic legitimation of rulers has solidified political order. Challenges to the State's monopoly of violence coming from within the

Table 6 State–democracy mechanisms and outcomes: advanced and Latin American countries

	Cases					
	Advanced countries, nineteenth to twentieth century			Latin American countries, 1980s–2010s		
Type of causal mechanism/causal mechanism	France	England/Britain	United States	Brazil	Mexico	Argentina
State-centered pro-democracy mechanisms						
• State building as the destruction of social elites opposed to democracy	✓		✓			
• State building as a driver of mass demand for democracy	✓	✓	✓			
State-centered anti-democracy mechanisms						
• State building as the destruction of social pluralism						
• State building as the empowerment of dictators						
• State building as the empowerment of State actors opposed to democracy				✓	✓	✓
Democracy-centered pro-state capacity mechanisms						
• Democratization as a basis of legitimation of the State	✓	✓	✓	✓	✓	✓
• Democratization as a source of politicians' incentives for state building	✓	✓	✓	≈	≈	≈
Outcome	– High-capacity democracy –			– Middle-quality institutional trap –		

Note: ✓ = Yes; ≈ = muted or weak; Blank = not salient.

State – such as the Brazilian Civil War of 1932 in which the state of São Paulo rebelled against the federal government – and from society – such as the insurgency of the late 1960s and early 1970s – are a thing of the past. However, democratization has failed to create either sustained mass demand or elite pressure for state building and the eradication of patrimonialism. The impact of traditional actors in politics has remained strong. To build legislative majorities, even the governments of Cardoso and the Workers Party (PT) have had to rely on parties closely tied to backward elites, such as the Brazilian Democratic Movement Party (PMDB). The low quality of Brazil's democracy has placed a limit on the incentives for state building that politicians face in a fully democratic regime (Unger 1990: 37–42, 351–74; Gomes and Unger 1996: 140–55).

Some of the failings of Brazil's democratic institutions have been compensated by the actions of social movements. However, the limits of this pressure on politicians are clear. Middle-class sectors in big cities have demanded an upgrade of state capacities. The demands have been more virulent after corruption scandals. Yet, expressions of frustration have been intermittent, eliciting some policy concessions at best but no major institutional reform. Politicians have responded to crises opportunistically and even cynically – doing only the minimum required to demobilize protests – rather than by building a consensus for a sweeping reform of the State (Taylor 2019). In other words, Brazil has opened a new chapter of the old story of "traditional politics against state transformation" (Hagopian 1994, 1996). As a result, elected officials seeking to show results to the electorate have responded by circumventing the permanent administration and creating "parallel bureaucracies" that are competent and loyal, but also unregulated (Grindle 2012: 150–51, 234–35). The more ambitious goal of making durable administrative reforms is sidestepped in the process.

On the other hand, the Brazilian State is a problem rather than a solution for democracy. Due to the patrimonial nature of the public administration, the State has been used by politicians for electoral purposes. One of the most egregious examples of such actions is the illegal funneling of kickbacks from a large construction company, Odebrecht, into election campaigns. Agents of the State have also used their rightful authority to intervene in politics in ways that are decidedly biased against the rule of law and democracy. The judiciary in Brazil has often provided impunity to corrupt politicians. It has also pursued a specific partisan agenda, such as the irregular intervention of the overzealous judge Sérgio Moro to disqualify Luiz Inácio "Lula" da Silva – the frontrunner in polls – from the presidential election of 2018 (Taylor 2019: 100–03). In addition, agents of the public administration act in a variety of ways, big and small, to undermine rather than strengthen universal citizenship (Caldeira and Holston 1999).

Thus, the failure to carry out a full-blown state reform is a source of weakness of democracy. The State has not undermined the power of traditional elites who resist democracy. Moreover, the arbitrary intervention of politicians in the administration and the politicization of the civil service turn the State into a site of resistance against democracy. Indeed, the patrimonial practices of the Brazilian State undermine democracy through direct interventions that bias the democratic process in favor of candidates specialized in the protection of oligarchic wealth and through the curtailment of a universal conception of citizenship.

The combination of mechanisms in operation in contemporary Brazil differs from those present in France, Britain, and the United States (see Table 6). The democratic legitimation of rulers has eliminated violent conflict over the regime and strengthened the State's monopoly of violence. However, pressures to build state capacity more broadly are muted, due to the low quality of democracy. Attempts to reform the State are crushed by the persistent power of traditional elites. They outweigh mass demand for administrative capacity and hence reduce the incentives politicians face to champion state reform. In turn, improvements in the quality of democracy are blocked by the lack of state capacity – in particular, the failure to eradicate patrimonial practices that ensure the persistence of undemocratic social elites and State agents. Brazil's middle-quality institutional trap has strong microfoundations.

4.2.2 Mexico

Mexico democratized in the 1990s and started its current democratic period with a medium degree of coercive capacity and a low degree of administrative capacity. Positive features of Mexico's post-2000 democracy are that the three main political parties have alternated in office, and that the party that had governed during most of the twentieth century, the PRI (Institutionalized Revolutionary Party), regained the presidency in 2012, lost the 2018 election, and peacefully transferred power to the winner. However, Mexican democracy is flawed, most obviously in that violence, big money, and large-scale corruption affect campaigns, electoral results, and policy-making (Córdova and Murayama 2006; Morris 2009; Bailey 2014; Cadena-Roa and López Leyva 2019). Additionally, many states are "authoritarian enclaves" that have a disproportionate weight in national level politics (Gibson 2012: ch. 5; Giraudy 2015: 39–44, ch. 7).

With regard to the public administration, a key achievement was the delinking of the PRI from the State. However, success at state reform has been elusive.

After democratizing, Mexico has not implemented a serious civil service reform. Indeed, its 2003 civil service reform had only a marginal long-term effect. Democratic rulers in 2000 inherited a patrimonial administration and have not made any substantial changes (Graham 1998; Grindle 2012: 189–95, 220–24). Additionally, since 2006 the State's inability to defeat challengers rooted in organized crime has rightly given Mexico the reputation of a fragile State and a violent democracy (Davis 2017). Mexico is far from attaining a high-capacity democracy. As in Brazil, progress has been stalled.

The mechanisms in operation in Mexico resemble those in Brazil. On the one hand, the democratic legitimation of rulers has eliminated challenges to the State's monopoly of violence that emerged in a context of authoritarian rule, such as the revolutionary forces in the 1910s and the guerrillas in the late 1960s and 1970s. Democratization also created a mass demand for public goods, and the civil service reform introduced in 2003 can be attributed to it. However, flaws in democracy have distorted mass demands and hence politicians have not had a clear incentive to provide public goods. Reform would require confronting entrenched interests within the State that have traditionally seen the administration as private property and resisted reform. Yet, elected politicians have been reluctant or unable to break with the old system of patronage. They simply adapted it to a democratic context: decisions about allocation of government jobs, made within the PRI in the twentieth century, have been cartelized among the main parties (Grindle 2012: 220–24).

On the other hand, the Mexican State is a problem rather than a solution for democracy. This is best grasped by focusing on the security services. The violence in twenty-first-century Mexico is different from the politically driven violence, fueled by a lack of democracy, in the twentieth century. Moreover, the current violence did not originate under democracy. Indeed, the Mexican drug cartels started to develop under authoritarian rule in the 1970s and 1980s. However, narco power grew under democracy. First, drug cartels exploited the weakness of a patrimonial State, gaining the complicity of the security forces and the judiciary, through bribes and intimidation. Then, more brazenly, they entered into politics through the front door – illegally funding candidates running for office, bribing elected rulers, and variously exploiting weaknesses in the democratic political regime – and escalated their use of violence – killing politicians, policemen, and judges who threatened the drug business and its spinoffs (contraband, human traffic, and ransom). Thus, the problem of the cartels and the attendant levels of violence is deeply rooted in Mexico's patrimonial administration. Even though the mass demand for order has been strong, elected rulers and State agents have colluded with organized crime for private and partisan gain. The inability of the State to eliminate the power of organized crime and, worse, the contribution of politicians and State agents to the creation of a parallel narco State have undermined democracy (Bailey 2014: 9–10, chs. 5 and 6). In Mexico, the State is a site of resistance to democracy.

In sum, the combination of mechanisms in operation in contemporary Mexico adds weight to the lessons from Brazil's post-1985 experience. Though advanced countries have shown that a high-capacity democracy can be built by following the coevolution path, Mexico's experience shows that the prospects of progress along that path is limited when flaws in the democratic regime weaken the demand for state building, and when agents within the State, whether acting alone or in concert with political leaders or organized crime, use their position to undermine political rights.

4.2.3 Argentina

Argentina democratized in the early 1980s and started its current democratic period with relatively high coercive capacity but only modest administrative capacity. Since 1983, Argentina has had an enduring democracy. However, as in Brazil and Mexico, its democracy has many flaws. Elected presidents have not ended their full term in office in 1989 and 2001. Corruption plays a big role in electoral campaigns and the policy-making process (Alconada Mon 2018). Provinces that are "authoritarian enclaves" have a role, often critical, in national politics (Gibson 2012: ch. 4; Giraudy 2015: 39–44, ch. 6). Argentina has a low-quality democracy.

With regard to the public administration, it embarked on two attempts to reform the State, in 1991–92 and 2002, and, again as in Brazil and Mexico, made some progress in building state capacity (Ferraro 2011: 165; Grindle 2012: 184–89, 215–20). However, these reforms failed to bring about a sustained and significant reduction of patrimonialism (Grindle 2012: 215–17; Panizza, Larraburu, and Scherlis 2018: 71–81). The practice of relying on parallel bureaucracies, as a way to deal with pressing policy challenges or circumventing career officials seen as loyal to prior rulers, has remained intact (Ferraro 2011: 161–64; Grindle 2012: 186, 219). Argentina is another Latin American case in which progress toward a high-capacity democracy has stalled.

The mechanisms in operation in Argentina also resemble those in Brazil and Mexico. Democracy has solidified political order by legitimating rulers. Thus, the country has overcome an important problem in its past, when challenges to the State's monopoly of violence came from within the State, as in the case of the confrontation between branches of the military in 1962–63, and from society, as in the case of the powerful guerrilla organizations that engaged in armed actions in the 1970s. Democracy has also created a mass demand for public goods, and the incentive for politicians to respond to citizen preferences by developing state capacity is evident in the reforms launched in 1991–92 and 2002.

However, mass demand for state building is translated into policy only inasmuch as politicians develop a long-term horizon and expect that alternation in power will soon place them in opposition. Only then is it rational for incumbents to relinquish the obvious short-term advantage of appropriating state resources for partisan goals. Yet, Argentina has not met this condition. Since 1983, alternations in power have been peaceful. However, all non-Peronist presidents failed to end their terms successfully, let alone win reelection. Indeed, the end of non-Peronist presidencies (in 1989, 2001, and 2019) has always been crisis-ridden, including major episodes of macroeconomic instability. Additionally, two out of three non-Peronist presidents could not finish their terms (1989 and 2001). Thus, for the key political actor in Argentina – the Peronists – democracy has still not created an incentive to reduce incumbency advantages by enacting a meritocratic civil service reform.

In addition, mass demand for state building is weakened because territorial politics distorts democracy – largely through provincial authoritarian enclaves – by introducing a conservative policy bias that involves a strong deviation from majority rule. In effect, territorial politics induces the national government to be less responsive to the preferences of the median voter and more to those of the median governor, which have no reason to coincide. Thus, democratic deficiencies, which block democracy's power to channel mass demand for state building, impede the formation of the political consensus needed to push through major and sustainable reforms of the public administration.

In turn, in Argentina, as in Brazil and Mexico, it is important to also consider State-centered mechanisms. The failure of the State to destroy intermediary powers – in particular, the territorially based actors who carve out quotas of political power and undermine political rights in various ways – has been an obstacle to full democratization. Additionally, the judiciary has become a caste that offers impunity to corrupt politicians (Alconada Mon 2018: introduction, chs. 12 and 13), and agents within the State, both at the national and subnational levels, undermine democratic citizenship by using public resources for partisan purposes and by refusing to enforce rights. The Argentine State is a site of resistance to democracy.

Argentina further underscores some distinctive features of Latin American politics. Democracy became the undisputed form of conflict resolution, inaugurating an unprecedented era of political peace and respect for human rights.

However, because democracy is flawed, the potential impact of democracy on state building is weakened. In turn, because the country has not carried out a transition to a bureaucratic administration, an improvement in the quality of democracy is blocked. Thus, in contemporary Argentina a weak democracy and a patrimonial administration reinforce each other.

4.3 Conclusions

The contrast between the combination of mechanisms in operation in cases that succeeded at building high-capacity democracies and in contemporary Latin America supports a key claim. Latin America is caught in a middle-quality institutional trap not because it has followed the wrong path – failing to follow the State-first path – but rather because of the mechanisms in play in the State–democracy interaction. The paths followed by Latin American countries are not different from the paths followed by Western European and other advanced countries. However, the specific combination of mechanisms through which the State affects democracy and democracy affects the State in Latin American countries is different from the combination of mechanisms that operated in Western European and other advanced countries.

What is distinctive about Latin America, and what offers a key clue to understanding why the region is caught in a middle-quality institutional trap, is its distinctive State–democracy dynamic. As the advanced countries show, States can make democracy and democracy can make States, when the State–democracy interaction is a virtuous cycle. However, in contemporary Latin America, flawed democracies have a muted effect on state reform and the failure to build a bureaucratic administration reproduces flawed democracies. The outcome is Latin America's middle-quality institutional trap.

5 Macroconditions of the State–Democracy Interaction

The analysis thus far has shown that the State–democracy interaction in contemporary Latin America is in a perverse, self-perpetuating equilibrium. State and regime institutions fall well short of the standard of a high-capacity democracy because low-quality democracies impede upgrades in state capacities, and patrimonial or semi-patrimonial States block an improvement in the quality of democracy. Latin America's middle-quality institutional trap has microfoundations. But, is this equilibrium robust, that is, resistant to perturbations? To address this question, we next look "outside the box" of the State–democracy interaction and consider whether the trap also has macrofoundations.

The macroconditions that shape the State–democracy interaction are likely to differ across regions and epochs. For example, the experience of foreign occupation following World War II played a role in Germany's and Japan's path to high-capacity democracies and will not repeat. The search for universal macro-level conditions of high-capacity democracies is unlikely to produce results. Thus, we focus on the macroconditions that are specifically relevant to contemporary Latin American politics.

The crux of the matter is whether a set of macroconditions support the reproduction of the mechanisms that underpin the current status quo or carry the potential to alter the mechanisms in operation (see Table 6, last three columns). Thus, (1) we consider how macroconditions shape and constraint the *power* and *preferences* of actors regarding the regime and the State, and (2) we link the power and preferences of actors to three *outcomes*: persistence of the status quo, progress, or regression.

Moreover, the point of the analysis is to check how robust Latin America's middle-quality institutional equilibrium is. In an exercise analogous to stress tests used to assess the resilience of financial institutions and robustness checks in regression analysis, we consider a broad range of plausible macro sources of disruption. The basic logic of this analysis is that the tougher the tests that are survived – the more numerous and credible the sources of potential disruption that fail to dislodge the equilibrium – the stronger are the grounds for claiming that Latin America's middle-quality institutional equilibrium is robust. To this end, we cast a wide net, considering a total of eight macroconditions that recur in the study of Latin American politics and that span different spheres.

To preview the analysis, we group the eight macroconditions into three categories (see Table 7). Some macroconditions empower actors who benefit from the status quo and thus actively sustain it. A second set of macroconditions makes actors who benefit from capacity building weak and thus blocks progress. Finally, a third set of macroconditions has induced a change in the regime preferences of strong actors who in the past had benefited from authoritarianism and thus prevent regression. Hence, as we elaborate next, Latin America's combination of flawed democracies and low-to-medium capacity States is a robust equilibrium.

5.1 Why the Status Quo Persists

The dual persistence of flawed democracies and low-to-medium capacity States is rooted, most fundamentally, in a range of macroconditions – some political and domestic, others economic and international – that empower actors who support the status quo. They want neither an improvement nor a deterioration of democracy or state capacity.

Table 7 A theory of high-capacity democracy: macroconditions of the State–democracy interaction in contemporary Latin America

Type of macrocondition/ macrocondition	Actor	Actor power	Actor preferences	Outcome
Status quo–sustaining macroconditions				
• Legacy of state formation	Subnational territorial rulers	Strong	Regime status quo State status quo	Persistent status quo Persistent status quo
• Political economy of twenty-first-century populism	Populist politicians	Strong	Regime status quo State status quo	Persistent status quo Persistent status quo
• Political economy of the global drug trade	Drug cartels	Strong	Regime status quo State status quo	Persistent status quo Persistent status quo
Progress-blocking macroconditions				
• Socioeconomic inequality	Middle class	Weak	Pro-reform of State	No progress
• Hierarchical capitalism	Independent business sector	Weak	Pro-reform of State	No progress
• Dependence on international finance	International financial agencies	Weak	Pro-reform of State	No progress
Regression-preventing macroconditions				
• International democracy regime	Political class	Strong	Regime status quo	No regress
• Economic globalization	Internationalized capitalist class	Strong	Regime status quo	No regress

5.1.1 The Legacy of State Formation

A key macrocondition of current politics in Latin America is a legacy of state formation in the nineteenth century (Mazzuca 2021; see also Foweraker 2018: ch. 4). In Latin America, in contrast to the pioneer cases of Western Europe, States were formed through a process of periphery incorporation that did not eliminate the patrimonial privileges of regionally based actors. Subnational territorial rulers not only survived the process of state formation but also obtained the institutional means to reproduce local power and a share of national power. State makers of large countries in Latin America typically incorporated peripheries by extending three types of institutional concessions: federalism, which allowed patrimonial rulers to entrench local control; a disproportionally powerful Senate, which secured patrimonial rulers a seat in key decision-making arenas; and cross-regional parties, which allowed provincial rulers to deliver blocks of captive votes in exchange for subsidies from the center. The political equilibrium in contemporary Latin America can be seen, in part, as the durable legacy of the process of state formation.

Patrimonial peripheral rulers are powerful actors in contemporary Latin America. To win elections and govern, coalitions must be put together, and such coalitions must include patrimonial territorial rulers. Indeed, governors of backward and thinly populated provinces are often pivotal actors. Moreover, these actors have well-defined preferences. Their regime preferences span a narrow range. On the one hand, they defend democracy because they have flourished under democracy and could lose access to a key prize, government offices, if democracy broke down. On the other hand, they benefit from the flaws of current democracies and thus resist improvements in its quality. In turn, their preferences about capacity building are straightforward. Subnational territorial rulers derive large benefits – levels of income and status they could never achieve in alternative professional paths – from patrimonial control over territorial bastions. The use of state resources for purposes of patronage plays an important role in ensuring continued electoral access to government offices and governability between elections. Thus, the fate of subnational territorial rulers is intimately linked with the patrimonialization of provincial administrations and with clientelistic linkages to the central State. They see any change of the large-scale patronage machinery as a threat to their survival. Subnational territorial rulers are a key factor in the stability of Latin America's middle-quality institutional arrangement.

Evidence about deviant cases within Latin America strengthens this argument. Uruguay and Costa Rica are two Latin American cases that have taken important steps to develop high-quality democracies and build state capacity.

Crucially, the process of state formation in these two countries is set apart from the rest of the region (Mazzuca 2021). State formation in Uruguay and Costa Rica was marked by two features: the absence of backward peripheries dominated by patrimonial lords and the leading role of political parties. Uruguay and Costa Rica are single-region countries with low population density, and the simplicity of the territorial basis exempted them from domination by patrimonial lords, able to command a large clientele of workers tied to the land and to become entrenched as subnational oligarchies. Furthermore, political conflict in Uruguay and Costa Rica was structured around political parties that were not able to inflict a decisive defeat to the each other. This foundational partisan stalemate was the source of a two-party system and political institutions that facilitated power sharing and conflict resolution. Thus, the distinctive process of state formation in these two countries put them on a path that helped them avoid the problems of democracy that are common in Latin America. In turn, the strength of democracy in Uruguay and Costa Rica has weakened an actor prone to resist state reform.

Democracy can be a means of State transformation, and a reform of the State can improve the quality of democracy. However, the power of subnational patrimonial rulers, a persistent political macrocondition that has become even stronger under democracy, makes the region's middle-quality institutions a stable arrangement. Actors who under democracy are in control of key levers of power do not have the motivation to alter the combination of flawed democracies and low-to-medium capacity States.

5.1.2 The Political Economy of Twenty-First-Century Populism

A second macrocondition sustaining the middle-quality institutional trap in Latin America is the political economy of populism in the twenty-first century. Due to the rise of China and India as global industrial superpowers and voracious consumers of raw materials, fossil fuels and proteins, the primary sector in Latin America underwent an unprecedented revival from 2003 to the mid-2010s, the magnitude of which is only comparable to the original export-led boom of growth of 1870–1910 (Wise 2020). And a new model of economic development based on natural resource extraction, sometimes referred to as "extractivism" or "neoextractivism" (Gudynas 2015; Svampa 2019), has had widespread negative implications for democracy (Mazzuca 2013).

The negative political consequences of extractivism have been most apparent in Venezuela under Chávez, Bolivia under Morales, and Ecuador under Correa – the so-called Bolivarian countries – together with Argentina under the Kirchners. All Latin American countries benefiting from the new commodity boom of the twenty-first century used the new fiscal resources to fund social policies of various kinds, a common denominator of which was consumption subsidies for the "precariat" – chronic unemployed and informal workers. One country, Chile, stood out by using the commodity windfall in an anti-cyclical fashion. Yet the Bolivarian cases and Argentina are a distinct group, in which economic populism eroded political democracy.[30]

On the economic side, the Bolivarian cases and Argentina secured for the State the lion's share of the torrential flow of revenues derived from the commodity boom, either by nationalization or semi-confiscatory taxation. Additionally, relying on a notable expansion of the size of the State, they incentivized consumption at the expense of investment, to the point that they even sought to maintain private consumption when the economy was shrinking. On the political side, the popularity dividend derived from economic populism allowed presidents to score electoral landslides, which in turn encouraged them to concentrate political power, increase the advantage of incumbency, use the public administration for private or partisan gain, and over time curtail such basic rights as free press and access to information – for example, by shutting down opposition media or intervening technical statistics offices. The political economy of twenty-first-century populism is an additional macrocondition of the middle-quality institutional trap and an impediment to the building of high-capacity democracies in Latin America.

However, it is also key to note that the political economy of twenty-first-century populism places limits on the erosion of democracy and does not raise the specter of democratic breakdowns led by a category of incumbents – left-leaning populist elected leaders – on anything like the scale of the anti-populist coups during the Cold War years. Populist leaders must maintain access to international commodity markets so as to bring in much-needed hard currency – thus, though Chávez did not lose an opportunity to score ideological points against US presidents, he always depended on selling Venezuelan oil to the United States – and are at the mercy of inherently volatile international commodity markets. Thus, the new populist presidents are extremely vulnerable to sudden downturns in international prices. At some point, economic populism ceases to be economically viable and its political dividends begin to exhaust. During good economic times, populist leaders seem unbeatable at the polls, and their repeated electoral victories are taken by some as a sign that democracy is

---

[30] We do not hereby indicate that the threats to democracy have only come from political leaders usually categorized as left populist leaders. See Munck (2015) on other sources of threat. Rather, we draw attention to a potential novelty, given that the breakdown of democracy in the twentieth century nearly always involved the military and frequently was carried out against populist elected leaders.

doomed. However, populist leaders risk electoral failure even in low-quality democracies and have shown a willingness to accept electoral defeat.

The breakdown of democracy in Venezuela under Maduro, after his electoral defeat in the parliamentary elections of 2015, shows that rulers may simply opt to abandon democracy when economic populism becomes electorally unviable. However, the case of Venezuela also shows why democratic breakdown is not likely in other countries led by populist presidents. The death of Venezuelan democracy is based on a large redistribution of political power from civilian politicians to security forces, a loss that few professional politicians elsewhere are willing to incur. Additionally, the breakdown seems viable only if some external actor, such as Russia and China, has geopolitical reasons to provide support, a rare circumstance. Finally, Venezuela under Maduro shows that breaking with democracy requires a high level of violence against political dissent, a risky bet in an age when the norm of transitional justice has gained ground. Thus, it is more rational for populist leaders to concede electoral defeat in hard economic times, let a right-wing force produce the economic adjustment and pay the attendant political cost, and administer their political capital from the opposition with a focus on the next election. Except for presidents who have to worry about prison at the end of their terms, abandoning democracy is too risky, especially for parties and movements with a track record of winning free and fair elections. In short, though the political economy of twenty-first-century populism is a reason why high-capacity democracies are unlikely in Latin America, it also explains why powerful actors do not support the breakdown of democracy.

5.1.3 The Political Economy of the Global Drug Trade

Another macrocondition of Latin America's middle-quality institutions is the global drug trade. Much as Latin America is inserted in the global economy as a producer of legal primary commodities, so too has it responded to the United States and European demand for illegal commodities – especially cocaine, methamphetamines, and heroin – since the 1970s. Latin America is the main world grower of coca leaves and producer of cocaine, a key player in the production of synthetic drugs, and a large hub for heroin imports into the United States. And Latin America's central role in the global drug trade has had a deleterious impact both on democracy and the State (Bailey 2014; Bagley and Rosen 2015; Durán-Martínez 2018; Yashar 2018).

The global drug trade strengthens certain actors – cartels specialized in the production and export of narcotics – that have a distinct basis of power. Drug cartels, especially those in Colombia (1980–2000) and Mexico (since 1990) put together formidable private armies and built large arsenals of sophisticated weapons. Drug cartels also have accumulated immense amounts of wealth and play a key role in the economy, especially at the local level. Moreover, the cartels' military and economic power is far from circumstantial. The US-sponsored "war against drugs" affects the location of drug production sites, but it does not affect the aggregate level of output; coca growing moves from one region to another. The war on drugs can also decapitate the most prominent cartels by capturing their leader, but a recurrent unintended consequence is the splintering of cartels into warring factions and the emergence of rival cartels of similar magnitude elsewhere. So long as the international demand for illegal drugs remains high, the overall power of drug cartels in Latin America will persist through re-localization and reorganization.

The impact of drug cartels on the democracy and the State is variegated and forceful. Fundamentally, with their military power, they challenge the State's monopoly of violence. More surreptitiously, given that drug cartels are underground organizations, they gain influence over regime and State actors who could affect their business through a mixture of threats and bribes. Drug cartels have distorted democratic politics by threatening and killing politicians and elected officeholders, and by illegally funding electoral campaigns and buying off elected representatives. Though it is difficult to measure the distortion that narco politics introduces in democratic representation, it is substantial, especially at the subnational level. Indeed, some elected representatives have specialized in protecting the wealth and activities of drug lords in exchange for a share of drug-trafficking revenues.

Furthermore, though drugs cartels have not captured the State, they have essentially used the propensity toward patrimonialism to ensure that the State does not work to deliver key public goods interfering with drug trafficking and instead allows them to run a range of illegal businesses. Drug cartels influence the civil service by bribing or intimidating judges. Drug cartels also influence the security apparatus, inducing elements within the police and the military to provide protection from attacks by rival cartels and by the non-corrupted portions of the security forces. It is not an exaggeration to state that drug cartels are a key political actor not only in Colombia and Mexico, but also in Central America, Peru, Brazil, Bolivia, Paraguay, and Argentina.

The preferences of drug cartels regarding the regime and the State are hard to discern. They clearly oppose an improvement of the quality of democracy and an increase in state capacity. These changes could not be brought about without harming the interest of drug cartels. However, it is plausible that drug cartels would be worse off with the breakdown of democracy and/or the weakening of state capacity. Drug cartels have been very successful within Latin America's middle-quality institutions. A change of the current situation entails risks and costs, which would force the drug cartels to seek new allies and device new strategies to protect their businesses. In short, the global drug trade is another macrocondition of Latin America's middle-quality institutions. It empowers actors who are opposed to high-capacity democracies and, more generally, favor the current status quo.[31]

5.2 Why No Progress?

A complementary reason for the endurance of patrimonial administrations is that three additional macroconditions – socioeconomic inequality, hierarchical capitalism, and dependence on international finance – make actors who would benefit from the bureaucratization of the public administration – and thus prefer a reform of the State – weak and relatively ineffectual.

5.2.1 Socioeconomic Inequality

Latin America tops the world ranking of inequality. This macrocondition is a key impediment to the reform of the State. In an unequal democracy, the median voter is a poor person, who creates an incentive for politicians to allocate fiscal resources to the creation of some form of income subsidy at the expense of the provision of public goods.[32] Unequal democracies reward patronage-based parties with extensive networks of brokers who use subsidies to the poor as a clientelistic mode of electoral mobilization (Stokes et al. 2013; Nichter 2018; Calvo and Murillo 2019). Thus, socioeconomic inequality is an additional factor that accounts for the failure of capacity building under democracy. The weakness of mass demand for States capable of delivering public goods is rooted in one of the region's most enduring features.

The flip side is that the same condition that makes the median voter a poor person accounts for the absence of a vibrant middle class. The middle class is the

---

[31] Another line of thinking worth pursuing is whether the drug trade might lead the military to push for a breakdown of democracy so as to respond to the security threat, as they did in the 1960s and 1970s. However, the threat to political order brought about by drug cartels is different than the threat of guerrilla organizations (they sought to take over the government) and the international environment is different from the Cold War environment (in Latin America, it is less permissive of military coups). Furthermore, democratic governments in Latin America are placing few limits on their security forces and collaborating rather extensively with the US Department of Defense. Thus, even though the drug trade has the potential of becoming a geopolitical issue that is considered as a threat by the US government, it is unlikely that it will lead to any major deviation from the current status quo.

[32] The frequently invoked Meltzer and Richard (1981) model assumes the operation of high-quality democracies and, as we have stressed, this assumption does not hold in Latin America. Indeed, democracy fails to channel a demand for state reforms in Latin America precisely because socioeconomic inequality undermines the quality of democracy.

key victim of patrimonialism. It shoulders its tax burden – it is systematically overtaxed in every large economy of Latin America – and receives few public goods in return (Avanzini 2012). In turn, two signature issues of concern that have mobilized the middle class are the failure of governments to end corruption at high levels of the government and State and to protect the population from criminal violence. Thus, the middle class could be an advocate of civil service reform (Bárcena and Serra 2010; Paramio 2010).[33] Yet, its relatively small numbers – some estimates puts it at between 20 and 25 percent of the region's population, others at 33 percent (Portes and Hoffman 2003: 52; Penfold and Rodríguez Guzmán 2014: 23) – and weak representation – few parties have built durable links to it (Di Tella 2004: ch. 8) – have limited its political effectiveness. Despite isolated protests against corruption and violence, middle-class social movements have proved extremely ephemeral.[34]

Latin American democracies are embedded in highly unequal societies. They are unequal democracies (Luna 2014). Thus, mass demand for state building is stifled. And the incentives for politicians to respond to crucial needs through capacity building reforms are weak (Kaufman and Nelson 2004). A key hope for progress – the possible channeling of demands for public goods through democracy – is dashed because the middle class, potentially a pro-reform actor, is weak.

5.2.2 Hierarchical Capitalism

The kind of capitalism is also important because it affects elite interest in a reform of the State. The economies of Latin American countries are examples of hierarchical capitalism (Schneider 2013). The business sector is concentrated, labor markets are segmented, and a major source of profits for domestic capitalists is business with the State or direct favors from the government. This economic structure has been persistent. Indeed, neoliberal reforms in the 1990s produced the irreversible death of the kind of State/capital relations that characterized import-substitution industrialization from the 1930s to the 1970s. It largely dismantled the protections to the formal sector of the workforce and allowed international firms to compete with national ones. Yet, hierarchical capitalism survived neoliberal reforms.

---

[33] See also Estache and Leipziger (2009), Daude and Melguizo (2010: 19), and Penfold and Rodríguez Guzmán (2014: 45–48). We hasten to add that, as research on the middle class's regime preferences shows (Rosenfeld 2017), we expect that their preference regarding state reform could be reduced if they are employed by the State.

[34] In Uruguay and Costa Rica, the absence of large inequalities has prevented polarization around incompatible economic ideologies and created an incentive for parties to compete for the pivotal voters that reward parties that deliver public goods. Thus, deviant cases within Latin America strengthen this argument about the link between economic inequality and demand for state reform.

In contemporary Latin America, large national firms have dominant positions in privatized sectors, from transportation to energy, as well as in the sale of construction and provision services to the government. Interaction with the government and the State is key to their business model. Despite privatization, several prices of the economy, and thereby asset valuations, are defined through an eminently political process. Often key decisions affecting their business are made in secret negotiations between the presidents' closest collaborators and the firm's lobbyists. Crony capitalism is a rather prominent feature in Latin America (Rettberg 2005; Hernández López 2012; Bull, Castellaci, and Kasahara 2014: ch. 8; North, Rubio, and Acosta 2020).

The effects of crony capitalism on the prospects of a reform of the State are rather direct. It produces a strong disincentive among the most power-ful actors in the economy for institutional change. A key part of the business sector is a beneficiary of state protection, profiting from politically sanctioned monopolies and lavish contracts with the government, and hence has no interest in genuine state reform (Manzetti and Blake 1996; Alconada Mon 2018: chs. 2 and 3; Casar and Ugalde 2019; Durand 2019). An important potential driver of anti-patronage reform, an independent business sector that benefits from a State that enforces transparent rules evenly, is weak in Latin America.

5.2.3 Dependence on International Finance

Another potential source of state reform, particularly relevant in contexts of dependent capitalism, is pressure from the international financial community. Since the 1990s, key organizations that Latin American governments turn to for external financing have moved beyond their earlier recommendations of state shrinking and have begun to emphasize anti-corruption initiatives, a merit-based civil service, and other measures that would root out patrimonialism (Lora 2007; Cortázar, Lafuente, and Sanginés 2014; World Bank 2017). Yet, counter to the view of progressive sectors who ritually complain about the power of international capital to force domestic reforms, external pressure for reform has been weak in Latin America.

Latin American countries recurrently face the need to attract foreign invest-ments or request foreign loans, in part due to the waste of fiscal resources caused by patrimonialism. International financial organizations such as the International Monetary Fund routinely attach conditionalities, which go beyond fiscal and monetary goals and involve institutional reform, to their loans. Yet these conditionalities are never strong enough to cause a real change in patrimonial practices.

To get an international loan, the typical Latin American government pursues two equally ineffective strategies of capability building. Sometimes they signal their willingness to reform by hiring a hyper-technocratic team of economists for the Treasury and the Central Bank, a decision that creates the appearance of a break with old habits, but falls well short of the long-term political effort that is needed to upgrade the civil service. Other times they pass a new civil service law making entrance more meritocratic, as part of an exercise in window dressing, only to subsequently accept its rollback or curtailment (Grindle 2012: 226–39).

The adage "pra inglês ver," which the Brazilian political elite of the 1830s coined for antislavery legislation that was deliberately designed not to be enforced, refers to a reality that has largely remained unchanged for two centuries. Since the return of democracies, Latin American governments have produced copious bodies of legislation promising reform that impress foreigners but do not change how things actually work. It is not that international financial institutions are cheated. They play the game because the incentive of program officers is career progress rather than structural reform. Officers score professional points by brokering deals, not by monitoring implementation.

Dependence on international finance has created some pressure for a reform of the State. Though the international financial community and international financial organizations in particular have various agendas, they have promoted much-needed reforms of the State. Nonetheless, their power to induce a reform as politically charged as the elimination of pervasive patrimonialism is meager. Some special circumstances excepted (Stone 2008), even if outside actors are committed to state reform, they simply do not have the staying power needed to see complex reforms through to completion and they are not able to substitute for the lack of strong domestic support for reform (Hunter and Brown 2000; Kaufman and Nelson 2004: 488–89).

5.3 Why No Regression?

Finally, on a slightly more positive note, fundamental changes in the macro-political and macroeconomic international conditions that led to civil–military coup coalitions in Latin America during much of the twentieth century support the persistence of minimally democratic regimes.

5.3.1 The New International Democracy Regime

One global change is the rise, since the end of the Cold War, of an international regime promoting democracy. This regime upholds the view that a country must show democratic credentials in order to be a legitimate player in the international arena. And Latin American professional politicians, powerful actors within the current democratic politics of the region, have felt the effect of this new international regime with particular strength (Levitsky and Way 2010: ch. 4; Mainwaring and Pérez-Liñán 2014: 45–46, ch. 7). Indeed, in a departure from the Cold War period, the majority of politicians concur that authoritarian rule would undermine the international standing of the country, with the attendant risk of becoming a political and financial pariah.

The experience of Venezuela, which became a dictatorship in 2016, has been instructive for the region. It confirms the existence of the new international regime. On the one hand, the international community treats breakdowns of democracy more seriously than cases of corruption or nepotism. On the other hand, challengers need extraordinary endowments, like large reserves of oil, to survive external pressure for a considerable time. Indeed, though the international community has thus far failed to get President Maduro to step aside, the case of Venezuela is a warning sign to would-be autocrats and their supporters. The global legitimacy of democracy dissuades new generations of political actors from attempting a democratic breakdown.

However, the limits of this international macrocondition should also be noted. Missions of election observation carried out by the Organization of American States (OAS) routinely note the incidence of electoral clientelism, the disproportionate effect of semilegal contributions to electoral campaigns, violence against candidates, and various other indicators of a low-quality democracy (OAS 2011: ch. 6). Under its Democratic Charter of 2001, the OAS also has a mandate to act when threats to democracy occur between elections, such as when presidents are removed before their term has been completed. Yet, short of blatant electoral fraud that alters the results of an election, the toppling of a democratically elected president with military involvement, or the full usurpation of the powers of an elected legislature, the OAS has not acted in a concerted manner (Heine and Weiffen 2015; Perina 2015). The international democracy regime is effective at preventing democratic regressions that lead to overtly authoritarian outcomes. At the same time, the international community does little to pressure Latin America's countries to improve the quality of their democracies and never isolates low-quality democracies.

5.3.2 The New Economic Globalization

Another global change is the sweeping changes in the structure of the global economy since the 1980s and 1990s, and the liberalization of world financial markets in particular (Garretón et al. 2004: ch. 3). The impact of economic globalization on the internationalized capitalist class is well understood. Owners of capital have seen their action space critically expanded with the rise of financial globalization. Capitalists who fear redistribution from a democratic government can now readily move assets outside national borders before social reforms affect property rights. Globalization reduces the costs of democracy to a powerful actor, giving internationally oriented capitalists the option to exit the democratic game rather than break it (Boix 2003 12–13; Acemoglu and Robinson 2006: ch. 10).

Moreover, the positive effect of economic globalization on democracy in Latin America is clear. The more internationalized sector of the capitalist class was a frequent opponent of democracy from the 1960s to the 1980s. More specifically, it was a key actor in the civil–military coalitions that toppled democratically elected governments and ushered in a wave of right-wing military regimes (O'Donnell 1981; Rueschemeyer, Stephens, and Stephens 1992: ch. 5; Bartell and Payne 1995; Schneider 2004: chs. 4, 6, and 7). Yet, it abandoned its old antidemocratic posture in the new era of economic globalization. Indeed, the reduction of the cost of democracy for this powerful actor is an important reason why democracy has been stable since the 1990s.

However, as in the case of the new international democracy regime, the limits of this macrocondition should also be noted. The internationalized sector of the capitalist class is not a powerful advocate of democracy and it probably does not believe in the intrinsic value of democracy. Rather, it simply finds Latin American existing democracies tolerable. Thus, the impact of economic globalization on democracy is positive because it has removed a powerful threat to democracy and thus prevented any serious regression of democracy. At the same time, internationally oriented capitalists accept democracy in Latin America only because of its low quality and would likely resist attempts to improve its quality (Huber and Stephens 1999: 772–80). Economic globalization has turned a powerful actor prone to support the breakdown of democracies into one that supports low-quality democracies.

5.4 Conclusions

The question posed at the opening of this section – Is the equilibrium between State and democracy in Latin America resistant to perturbations? – can now be answered in light of this stringent test, which has addressed eight basic macro-conditions and considered whether any of them might disrupt this equilibrium. Moreover, a rather categorical answer can be offered.

The State–democracy interaction in Latin America has generated a self-perpetuating equilibrium, and an analysis of macroconditions that could potentially upset this equilibrium point in the direction of the same conclusion: this equilibrium is robust. The actors benefiting from Latin America's political stagnation are very powerful, whereas the actors hurt by it and who prefer progressive reform are distinctly weak. The current equilibrium in Latin America has a bright spot: multiple macroconditions make the breakdown of democracy unlikely. However, various macroconditions also entrench the status quo and block the possibility of a virtuous cycle, in which democracy leads to building state capacity and capacity building leads to improvements in democracy. Given the current macroconditions, no actor interested in improving democracy or upgrading capacity is powerful enough to produce change. Latin America's middle-quality institutional trap has strong macrofoundations.

6 Concluding Remarks

The standard vision of Latin American politics and society has emphasized two macro-processes: economic development, on the one hand, and regime change – democratization in particular – on the other. The classic works and key debates have focused on these two processes and their interrelation. The relationship between the State and democracy has recently gained some attention. Nonetheless, relatively little is known about state formation and building, and the linkage between capacity building and regime change.

One influential proposal to reshape the standard vision about Latin American politics brings the State in under the form of a precondition. In this view, Latin America has failed to build high-capacity democracies because it has not followed the State-first European path, which allegedly developed state capacity before even toying with democracy. Latin America's problem is that it democratized prematurely. Yet, this diagnosis is wrong. Much as modernization theorists in the 1960s misunderstood economic development in Europe, so too do advocates of the State-first thesis rely on an invalid understanding of political development in Europe. It is not the case that all successful cases in Europe built capable States before democratizing, and it is not the case that Latin America has failed to build high-capacity democracies because it has not followed the European State-first model.

Multiple paths can lead to a high-capacity democracy and the difference between the paths followed by advanced countries and Latin America is not substantial. Thus, to understand the difference between advanced countries and Latin America, it is necessary to address the key puzzle that countries can follow a similar path yet reach a different outcome. Solving this puzzle requires studying the mechanisms operating at the levels of the State and the political regime. Some mechanisms lead to a virtuous self-reinforcing cycle and others do not – they might lead to a vicious cycle or create a self-perpetuating trap.

The distinctiveness of Latin America, compared to Western European and other advanced countries, and the reason why Latin America has not built high-capacity democracies, can thus be recast in the following terms.

States can make democracy and democracy can make States. More precisely, state building can foster democracy by destroying antidemocratic social elites and by fueling mass demand for political rights. In turn, democratization can lead to increases in state capacity by legitimating the State and by creating an incentive for competing politicians to deliver public goods. Thus, the starting point – whether countries develop state capacity first or democracy first – is less important than whether the State–democracy relation involves causal mechanisms that form a virtuous cycle. However, States make democracy and democracy makes States only under certain macroconditions, which trigger the causal mechanisms that make the State–democracy interaction a virtuous cycle.

In Latin America, the State–democracy interaction has not generated a virtuous cycle. Rather, it has generated a self-perpetuating arrangement that provides microfoundations to the region's middle-quality institutional trap. State failures leave the power of undemocratic social elites intact and grant power to State actors who undermine the quality of democracy. In turn, problems of democracy dampen the incentive for politicians competing in a democratic regime to reform the state. Thus, Latin America's combination of low-to-medium capacity States and flawed democracies is locked in. Moreover, a range of macroconditions make the State–democracy equilibrium robust. Powerful actors support the status quo. And no actor who would benefit from change is powerful enough to overcome status quo forces. Latin America's middle-quality institutional trap is a robust equilibrium.

Just as Latin America has experienced critical junctures that altered its path of political development in the past, so too will the current political equilibrium undergo change. Change could start with small steps taken by actors who exploit the possibility of sequential, part-by-part reforms that lead to big change, as suggested by Albert Hirschman in his reflections on revolutionary reformers (Hirschman 1963: ch. 5; see also Unger 1987 and O'Donnell 1998). The catalyst of change, however, will most likely be a shock that radically alters the macroconditions of current Latin American politics. Yet, only inasmuch as actors understand the current equilibrium will they be attuned to serious disequilibria, not mistake them with the many superficial changes that routinely occur, and not be taken by surprise by real change. Also, only inasmuch as this change is managed by actors who support the fuller democratization of political regimes and the building of capable States will Latin America make progress toward a high-capacity democracy.

Appendix
Concepts

The key concept in this manuscript, high-capacity democracy, is a composite concept constructed by combining state capacity and democracy. The concepts of State and democracy are defined in the literature in multiple, somewhat confusing and noncompatible ways. Thus, we start by clarifying how we conceptualize the modern State, state capacity, democracy, and how we draw on these concepts to form the concept of high-capacity democracy.[1]

State and Society

The modern State is an entity that is differentiated from society, and relates to society in two ways (see Figure A1). On the one hand, the *modern State* acts upon *society* through two means of *state capacity*: the *security services* (including the military and the police) and the *civil service* (aka the public administration). On the other hand, society accedes to the *government* of the modern State through the *political regime*, one basic option being a *democratic regime*. These distinctions are foundational in that they clarify the meaning of key political notions by specifying how concepts stand in relation to each other. However, the meaning and usefulness of this sketch only become apparent inasmuch as its core concepts and other related concepts are elucidated.[2]

---

[1] We address these conceptual matters because, as various authors have noted, the literature on the State and democracy is hampered by conceptual and terminological confusion (He 2001: 99; Bratton and Chang 2006: 1061–63; Mazzuca 2010: 340–42; Møller and Skaaning 2011: 2–6; Munck 2016: 2–10). Concerning terminology, though an earlier literature clearly distinguishes between *state* formation and *nation* building (Nettl 1968; Rokkan 1970: 54; 1975: 567), some recent works use these terms interchangeably or subsume both under the concept of nation building. In particular, a considerable amount of research uses nation building to refer to basic aspects both of nation building (e.g., the sense of national identity) and of state formation (e.g., the matter of territorial boundaries) (Rustow 1970: 350–52). More problematically, this literature suffers from conceptual confusion. In some works, the distinctiveness of the State and democracy is not clear. For example, Mann (2008: 356–57) conceptualizes democracy alternatively as a "type of regime" and a "type of state" that rates high on infrastructural power and low on despotic power. In other works, the difference between conceptual and causal statements is not clear. For example, Linz and Stepan's (1996a: 17–18, 28, 1996b: 14) phrase "no state, no democracy" could be taken as a purely conceptual claim – "democracy is a form of governance of a modern state" (Linz and Stepan 1996b: 17) – or as a causal statement that could be true or false. Thus, an elucidation of key concepts is needed.

[2] In this task, we draw on numerous scholars, including Weber (1946 [1919]: 77–82), Tilly (1990: 1–2), Mann (1993: 54–56), and Finer (1997a: 2–3) on the modern State; and Dahl (1971) and Bobbio (1986 [1984]) on democracy.

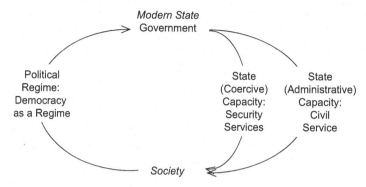

Figure A1 State, state capacity, and democracy: a sketch of a conceptual framework

Modern State and State Capacity

A modern State is a unique organization that exercises power over a society, a territorially circumscribed population or, more specifically, an organization in which a government, understood as the set of holders of high public office, acts upon society through its control of the security services that operate the means of coercion and of the civil service that manages the means of public administration.[3] Seen from a developmental perspective, a modern State comes into being through a process of territorial consolidation that involves the dual concentration of the means of coercion and the means of administration in the hands of a central authority. Thus, there is no modern State without a central government endowed with the capacity needed to govern over a bounded territory and the population contained within its borders and, more precisely, without the coercive capacity needed to sustain international sovereignty, suppress internal threats to its sovereignty, and enforce its commands, usually laws. Relatedly, no modern State exists without the administrative capacity needed to extract the resources to fund its coercive capacity.[4] In brief, there is no modern State without basic coercive and extractive capacities.

Nonetheless, beyond a minimal threshold, modern States may vary in terms of their capacity. The monopolization of violence is a necessary

---

[3] Here we follow Weber (1946 [1919]: 77–78), who argues that, since the State can have innumerable goals, from raising taxes and running prisons to delivering postal mail and producing steel and copper, a definition of the State should focus on its distinctive means. In turn, the distinction between security and civil services is standard in the literature; see, for example, Weber (1978 [1922]: 1393, 1399), Finer (1997a: 2–3), and Fukuyama (2011: 480).

[4] This idea is conveyed in S.E. Finer's (1975: 95) notion of a coercion–extraction–coercion cycle.

property of the State. Hence, the formation of modern States typically involves defeating and disarming private armies, and one of the key steps in state building is the creation of a permanent army that can deter challengers. However, modern States can be more or less effective in attaining and maintaining the monopoly of violence over time, and this core state capacity can erode short of complete State failure. Moreover, to maintain order over time, governments have to regularly innovate and reform their security services, as new challenges to the State's monopoly of violence emerge. In studying state capacity, it is important to address coercive capacity as a distinctive type of capacity and to distinguish the extent to which a State has coercive capacity.

Modern States also can vary a great deal in terms of their administrative capacity. To be successful at territorial consolidation, rulers have to develop some basic administrative capacity, so as to be able to raise funds through taxation. However, public administrations vary a lot in terms of their capacity to deliver public goods, a key reason being whether they are *patrimonial* or *bureaucratic administrations*.[5] In patrimonial administrations, rulers appropriate public resources for private or partisan gains, and patronage, nepotism, and corruption are common. In stark contrast, in bureaucratic administrations a distinction between politics and administration is maintained, and public and private or partisan roles are clearly separated. In bureaucratic administrations, governments accept that they only appoint a few top-level officials and that access to jobs and promotions in the public administration is largely based on exams and is merit-based. Additionally, in bureaucratic administrations, officials serve public goals determined by the government (Weber 1978 [1922]: chs. 11–13).[6] Thus, in studying state capacity, it is also important to address administrative capacity as

---

[5] Modern States also vary considerably in terms of their development of new functions, for example, in the economic and social arenas. Thus, studies of state capacity conventionally distinguish States in terms of their size and scope (e.g., amount of taxes raised, number of public employees, number of State functions). Additionally, modern States vary in the extent to which administrators are granted autonomy in decision-making, an issue emphasized in the literature on the New Public Management (Bresser-Pereira 2004). Without dismissing the importance of these distinctions, here we focus on the distinction between patrimonial and bureaucratic administrations as a central concern, of continued relevance in contemporary Latin America.

[6] The relationship between a government and a bureaucratic administration is complex and might be conveyed by the idea of accountable autonomy. On the one hand, this means that the administration is not subject to arbitrary intervention from the political powers and has autonomy with regard to appointments and promotions. On the other hand, this means that the administration is accountable to the government, which gives general directives to and exercises control over the administration, and is neither self-serving nor captured by societal actors.

a distinctive type of capacity and to distinguish between patrimonial and bureaucratic administrations.[7]

Political Regime and Democracy

Modern States also vary in terms of their political regime, the means of access to the government offices that are endowed with State power. The key distinction between political regimes is that between democracy and dictatorship (Bobbio 1989 [1985]), the distinctiveness of democracy being that it is a political regime in which access to government offices is regulated by the right to an elected government, the right to vote, and the right to run for office – a basic threshold being that elections for top national-level public offices are conducted with suffrage extending beyond the elites and without proscriptions of key parties or leaders – and removal from government office respects the right to complete constitutionally mandated terms in office. However, to clarify the concept of democracy, two additional points must be made.[8]

First, it is important to recognize that the concept of democracy can be used to distinguish both regime types and degrees of democracy. The concept of democracy is conventionally used, jointly with the idea of a threshold between democracy and dictatorship, to distinguish countries that are minimally democratic from those that belong in the category of dictatorship. However, just as it is crucial to distinguish democracies from dictatorships, it is also key to distinguish regimes that, having fulfilled the minimal requirements to be a democracy, reach different levels of democratic quality. Indeed, a distinction between low-quality and high-quality democracies can be made based on several criteria, such as the extension of the suffrage, electoral fraud, vote buying, electoral proscriptions, the use of violence in campaigns, the undue use of money (private or public) in elections, gross deviations from the principle of proportional representation, restrictions on the power of elected officeholders by unelected actors, and many more.

Second, it is crucial to avoid treating democracy as a property of the State. The idea of access to government offices is not meant to be understood in a restrictive way, such that a regime is characterized as democratic simply when the winners of democratic elections formally take office. The concept of access to government offices means, more fully, that the government offices accessed through democratic elections are endowed with the power to make legally binding decisions that are to

---

[7] As Weber (1978 [1922]: 981) notes, one could refer to a bureaucratic as opposed to a patrimonial army, and the bureaucratization of the army. For sake of terminological clarity, we use the term "bureaucratization" nearly exclusively in the context of the civil administration.

[8] For a fuller discussion of various conceptual issues regarding democracy, which touches on current discussions about the quality of democracy, see Munck (2016).

be executed by State agents (i.e., political decisions are not made by the civil or military officialdom, or some interest group that captures the State).[9] Thus, democracy is about where political power lies – or who has power – and even requires a certain relationship between the regime and the State – a regime is democratic when the power to direct the State is held by a government that is accessed democratically. However, democracy is a property of the political regime and not of the State.[10]

High-Capacity Democracy

Having clarified the concepts of modern State, state capacity, political regime, and democracy – and made the case for treating stateness and democraticness as different properties – the concept of high-capacity democracy can be defined as follows: high-capacity democracy is a compound concept that combines high state

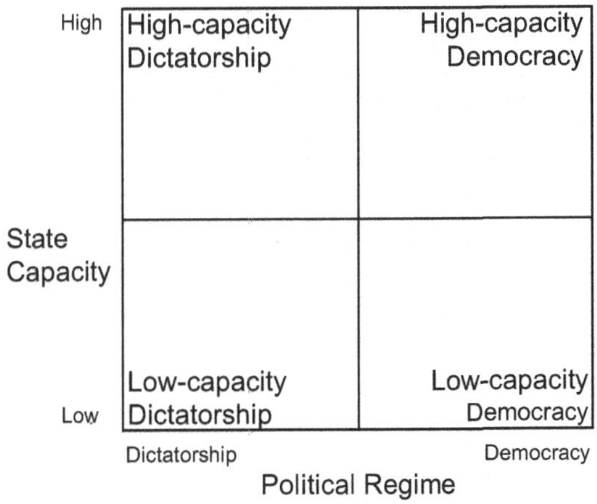

High	High-capacity Dictatorship	High-capacity Democracy
State Capacity		
Low	Low-capacity Dictatorship	Low-capacity Democracy
	Dictatorship	Democracy
	Political Regime	

Figure A2 State capacity and democracy: conceptual dimensions
Note: The dividing line on the *x* axis indicates the qualitative break between dictatorship and democracy, and the dividing line on the *y* axis indicates the qualitative break between patrimonial and bureaucratic security and civil services.

---

[9] This point is explicitly made by theorists of democracy in their conceptualizations of democracy. For example, in their definitions of democracy, Rokkan (1970: 79) includes executive power or cabinet responsibility, Schmitter and Karl (1991: 9) include civilian control over the military, and O'Donnell (2001: 13, 2010: 30–32) includes the more general criterion that "elections must be decisive" in the sense that elected officials "can actually make the binding decisions that a democratic constitutional framework normally authorize."

[10] To be more precise, since the political regime is, strictly speaking, the political regime of the State, democracy could be seen indirectly as a property of the State. However, democracy is a property of the government of the State and not of the State's security services and/or civil service.

capacity – in its coercive and administrative dimensions – and high-quality democracy. Indeed, simplifying matters, it is useful to rely on a two-dimensional conceptual space that graphically represents the concept of high-capacity democracy as the combination of two properties: high state capacity and high-quality democracy (see Figure A2).[11]

---

[11] This way of framing research on the State and democracy differs from the approach favored by O'Donnell (2001: 19–25, 2010: 28, ch. 11) and much of the recent literature on the quality of democracy (Ringen 2007: ch. 1; Morlino 2011: chs. 7 and 8), in that these authors include properties of the State in their definition of democracy (Mazzuca 2010: 335–44; Munck 2016). A case can be made that some aspects of state capacity might be constitutive of democracy – there are clearly limiting situations in which democracy cannot exist without a State capable of enforcing political rights. But we do not think this issue has been addressed clearly, let alone resolved, and thus we do not prematurely foreclose avenues for research regarding the relationship between the State and democracy. In turn, our concept of high-capacity democracy is very similar to Tilly's (2007: 17) identically named concept and Norris's (2012: 39) concept of bureaucratic democracies, and has some resemblance to North, Wallis, and Weingast's (2009) concept of open access orders and Acemoglu and Robinson's (2016, 2019) concepts of inclusive political institutions and shackled Leviathan. See also Ertman (1997: 6–10) for a similar conceptual framing.

References

Acemoglu, Daron and James A. Robinson. 2006. *Economic Origins of Dictatorship and Democracy.* New York, NY: Cambridge University Press.

2016. "Paths to Inclusive Political Institutions," in Jari Eloranta, Eric Golson, Andrei Markevich, and Nikolaus Wolf, eds., *Economic History of Warfare and State Formation.* Singapore: Springer, pp. 3–50.

2019. *The Narrow Corridor: States, Societies, and the Fate of Liberty.* New York, NY: Penguin.

Acemoglu, Daron, Suresh Naidu, Pascual Restrepo, and James A. Robinson. 2015. "Democracy, Redistribution, and Inequality," in Anthony Atkinson and François Bourguignon, eds., *Handbook of Income Distribution.* Vol. 2. Amsterdam: Elsevier, pp. 1885–966

Albertus, Michael and Victor Menaldo. 2012. "Coercive Capacity and the Prospects for Democratization." *Comparative Politics* 19(2): 151–69.

2018. *Authoritarianism and the Elite Origins of Democracy.* New York, NY: Cambridge University Press.

Alconada Mon, Hugo. 2018. *La raíz (de todos los males). Cómo el poder montó un sistema para la corrupción y la impunidad en la Argentina.* Buenos Aires: Planeta.

Anderson, Eugene N. and Pauline R. Anderson. 1967. *Political Institutions and Social Change in Continental Europe in the Nineteenth Century.* Berkeley, CA: University of California Press.

Arias, Enrique Desmond and Daniel M. Goldstein, eds., 2010. *Violent Democracies in Latin America.* Durham, NC: Duke University Press.

Arjona, Ana. 2016. *Rebelocracy: Social Order in the Colombian Civil War.* New York, NY: Cambridge University Press.

Auyero, Javier and Katie Sobering. 2019. *The Ambivalent State: Police-Criminal Collusion at the Urban Margin.* Oxford: Oxford University Press.

Avanzini, Diego. 2012. "Clase media y política fiscal en América Latina." *Serie Macroeconomía del Desarrollo* No 123. Santiago, Chile: CEPAL.

Aylmer, G. E. 1979. "Bureaucracy," in Peter Burke, ed., *The New Cambridge Modern History.* Vol. 13: *Companion Volume.* New York, NY: Cambridge University Press, pp. 164–200.

Bagley, Bruce M. and Jonathan D. Rosen, eds., 2015. *Drug Trafficking, Organized Crime, and Violence in the Americas Today.* Gainesville, FL: University Press of Florida.

Bailey, John. 2014. *The Politics of Crime in Mexico: Democratic Governance in a Security Trap*. Boulder, CO: First Forum Press.

Bárcena, Alicia and Narcís Serra, eds., 2010. *Clases medias y desarrollo en América Latina*. Santiago, Chile: CEPAL/CIDOB.

Barker, Ernst. 1944. *The Development of Public Services in Western Europe, 1660–1930*. New York, NY: Oxford University Press.

Bartell, Ernest and Leigh A. Payne, eds., 1995. *Business and Democracy in Latin America*. Pittsburgh, PA: University of Pittsburgh Press.

Bartolini, Stefano. 2000. *The Political Mobilization of the European Left, 1860–1980: The Class Cleavage*. New York, NY: Cambridge University Press.

Behrend, Jacqueline and Laurence Whitehead, eds., 2016. *Illiberal Practices: Territorial Variance within Large Federal Democracies*. Baltimore, MD: Johns Hopkins University Press.

Bellin, Eva. 2012. "Reconsidering the Robustness of Authoritarianism in the Middle East: Lessons from the Arab Spring." *Comparative Politics* 44(2): 127–49.

Bendix, Reinhard. 1964. *Nation-Building and Citizenship: Studies of Our Changing Social Order*. New York, NY: John Wiley & Sons.

Berman, Sheri. 2019. *Democracy and Dictatorship in Europe: From the Ancien Régime to the Present Day*. New York, NY: Oxford University Press.

Bersch, Katherine. 2019. *When Democracies Deliver: Governance Reform in Latin America*. New York, NY: Cambridge University Press.

Bersch, Katherine, Sérgio Praça, and Matthew Taylor. 2017. "Bureaucratic Capacity and Political Autonomy within National States: Mapping the Archipelago of Excellence in Brazil," in Miguel A. Centeno, Atul Kohli, and Deborah J. Yashar, eds., *States in the Developing World*. New York, NY: Cambridge University Press, pp. 157–83.

Bezes, Philippe and Martin Lodge. 2011. "The Development and Current Features of the French Civil Service System," in F. M. van der Meer, ed., *Civil Service Systems in Western Europe*. Cheltenham, MA: Edward Elgar, pp. 185–216.

Bien, David D. and Raymond Grew. 1978. "France," in Raymond Grew, ed., *Crises of Political Development in Europe and the United States*. Princeton, NJ: Princeton University Press, pp. 219–70.

Bilinski, Adam. 2018. "Paths to Democracy and Authoritarianism in Europe before World War One." *Journal of Historical Sociology* 31(4): 382–404.

Bobbio, Norberto. 1986 [1984]. *El futuro de la democracia*. Mexico: Fondo de Cultura Económica.

　　1989 [1985]. *Estado, gobierno y sociedad. Por una teoría general de la política*. Mexico: Fondo de Cultura Económica.

Boix, Carles. 2003. *Democracy and Redistribution*. New York, NY: Cambridge University Press.

Braddick, Michael. 2000. *State Formation in Early Modern England, c. 1550–1700*. Cambridge: Cambridge University Press.

Bratton, Michael and Eric C. C. Chang. 2006. "State Building and Democratization in Sub-Saharan Africa. Forwards, Backwards, or Together?" *Comparative Political Studies* 39(9): 1059–83.

Bresser-Pereira, Luiz Carlos. 2004. *Democracy and Public Management Reform: Building the Republican State*. Oxford: Oxford University Press.

Brewer, John. 1990. *The Sinews of Power: War, Money, and the English State, 1688–1783*. Cambridge, MA: Harvard University Press.

Brinks, Daniel M., Steven Levitsky, and Maria Victoria Murillo. 2019. *Understanding Institutional Weakness: Power and Design in Latin American Institutions*. New York, NY: Cambridge University Press.

Bull, Benedicte, Fulvio Castellaci, and Yuri Kasahara. 2014. *Business Groups and Transnational Capitalism in Central America: Economic and Political Strategies*. New York, NY: Palgrave Macmillan.

Cadena-Roa, Jorge and Miguel A. López Leyva, eds., 2019. *El malestar con la representación en México*. Mexico: IIS-CEIICH-UNAM.

Caldeira, Teresa P. R. and James Holston. 1999. "Democracy and Violence in Brazil." *Comparative Studies in Society and History* 41(4): 691–729.

Calvo, Ernesto and Maria Victoria Murillo. 2019. *Non-Policy Politics: Richer Voter, Poorer Voter, and the Diversification of Parties' Electoral Strategies*. New York, NY: Cambridge University Press.

Capoccia, Giovanni and R. Daniel Kelemen 2007. "The Study of Critical Junctures: Theory, Narrative, and Counterfactuals in Historical Institutionalism." *World Politics* 59(3): 341–69.

Caramani, Daniele. 2000. *Elections in Western Europe Since 1815: Electoral Results by Constituencies*. London: Macmillan Reference.

2004. *The Nationalization of Politics: The Formation of National Electorates and Party Systems*. New York, NY: Cambridge University Press.

Carbone, Giovanni, and Vencenzo Memoli. 2015. "Does Democratization Foster State Consolidation? Democratic Rule, Political Order, and Administrative Capacity." *Governance* 28(1): 5–24.

Cardoso, Fernando H. and Enzo Faletto. 1969. *Dependencia y desarrollo en América Latina*. Mexico: Siglo XXI.

Casar, María Amparo and Luis Carlos Ugalde. 2019. *Dinero bajo la mesa: Financiamiento y gasto ilegal de las campañas políticas en México*. Barcelona: Grijalbo.

Cavalcante, Pedro and Paulo Carvalho. 2017. "The Professionalization of Brazilian Federal Bureaucracy (1995–2014): Advances and Dilemmas." *Revista de Administração Pública* 51(1): 1–26.

Centeno, Miguel A. 2002. *Blood and Debt: War and the Nation-State in Latin America*. University Park, PA: Pennsylvania State University Press.

Centeno, Miguel A. and Agustin E. Ferraro, eds., 2013. *State and Nation Making in Latin America and Spain: Republics of the Possible*. New York, NY: Cambridge University Press.

Centeno, Miguel Angel and Fernando López-Alves, eds., 2001. *The Other Mirror: Grand Theory through the Lens of Latin America*. Princeton, NJ: Princeton University Press.

Childs, John. 2001. *Warfare in the Seventeenth Century*. London: Cassell.

Coleman, James Samuel. 1986. "Social Theory, Social Research, and a Theory of Action." *The American Journal of Sociology* 91(6): 1309–35.

Collier, David, ed., 1979. *The New Authoritarianism in Latin America*. Princeton, NJ: Princeton University Press.

Collier, Ruth Berins. 1999. *Paths Toward Democracy: Working Class and Elites in Western Europe and South America*. New York, NY: Cambridge University Press.

Collier, Ruth Berins and David Collier. 1991. *Shaping the Political Arena: Critical Junctures, the Labor Movement, and Regime Dynamics in Latin America*. Princeton, NJ: Princeton University Press.

Córdova, Lorenzo and Ciro Murayama. 2006. *Elecciones, dinero y corrupción: Pemexgate y Amigos de Fox*. Mexico: Cal y Arena.

Cortázar, Juan Carlos, Mariano Lafuente, and Mario Sanginés, eds., 2014. *Al servicio del ciudadano. Una década de reformas del servicio civil en América Latina-(2004–13)*. Washington, DC: Inter-American Development Bank.

Craver, Carl F. and Lindley Darden. 2013. *In Search of Mechanisms: Discoveries across the Life Sciences*. Chicago, IL: University of Chicago Press.

Croissant, Aurel and Olli Hellmann. 2020. "Stateness and Democracy: Evidence from Asia and Cross-regional Comparisons," in Aurel Croissant and Olli Hellmann, eds., *Stateness and Democracy in East Asia*. New York, NY: Cambridge University Press, pp. 233–62.

Daalder, Hans. 1966. "Parties, Elites, and Political Development in Western Europe," in Joseph LaPalombara and Myron Weiner, eds., *Political Parties and Political Development*. Princeton, NJ: Princeton University Press, pp. 43–78.

2011 [1995]. "Paths Toward State Formation in Europe: Democratization, Bureaucratization, and Politicization," in Hans Daalder, ed., *State*

Formation, Parties and Democracy: Studies in Comparative European Politics. Colchester: ECPR Press, pp. 33–48.

Dahl, Robert A. 1971. *Polyarchy: Participation and Opposition*. New Haven, CT: Yale University Press.

2003. *How Democratic Is the American Constitution?* 2nd ed. New Haven, CT: Yale University Press.

Daly, Sarah Zukerman. 2016. *Organized Violence after Civil War: The Geography of Recruitment in Latin America*. New York, NY: Cambridge University Press.

D'Arcy, Michelle and Marina Nistotskaya. 2017. "State First, Then Democracy: Using Cadastral Records to Explain Governmental Performance in Public Goods Provision." *Governance* 30(2): 193–209.

Dargent, Eduardo, Andreas E. Feldmann, and Juan Pablo Luna. 2017. "Greater State Capacity, Lesser Stateness: Lessons from the Peruvian Commodity Boom." *Politics and Society* 45(1): 3–34.

Daude, Christian and Ángel Melguizo. 2010. "Taxation and More Representation? On Fiscal Policy, Social Mobility and Democracy in Latin America," OECD Development Centre *Working Papers* 294. Paris: OECD Development Centre.

Davis, Diane. 2017. "Violence, Fragmented Sovereignty, and Declining State Capacity: Rethinking the Legacies of Developmental Statism in Mexico," in Miguel A. Centeno, Atul Kohli, and Deborah J. Yashar, eds., *States in the Developing World*. New York, NY: Cambridge University Press, pp. 63–92.

Dewey, Matías. 2015. *El orden clandestino: Política, fuerzas de seguridad y mercados ilegales en la Argentina*. Buenos Aires: Katz Editores.

Di Tella, Torcuato S. 2004. *History of Political Parties in Twentieth-century Latin America*. New Brunswick, NJ: Transaction Publishers.

Drake, Paul. 2009. *Between Tyranny and Anarchy: A History of Democracy in Latin America, 1800–2006*. Stanford, CA: Stanford University Press.

Durán-Martínez, Angélica. 2018. *The Politics of Drug Violence: Criminals, Cops and Politicians in Colombia and Mexico*. New York, NY: Oxford University Press.

Durand, Francisco. 2019. *Odebrecht: La empresa que capturaba gobiernos*. Lima, Peru: Fondo Editorial de la PUCP.

Eaton, Kent. 2017. *Territory and Ideology in Latin America: Policy Conflicts between National and Subnational Governments*. New York, NY: Oxford University Press.

Eaton, Kent and Juan Diego Prieto. 2017. "Subnational Authoritarianism and Democratization in Colombia: Divergent Paths in Cesar and Magdalena," in Tina Hilgers and Laura Macdonald, eds., *Violence in Latin America and the Caribbean: Subnational Structures, Institutions, and Clientelist Networks*. New York, NY: Cambridge University Press, pp. 153–72.

Elster, Jon. 2015. *Explaining Social Behavior: More Nuts and Bolts for the Social Sciences*, 2nd ed. New York: Cambridge University Press.

Ersson, Svante. 1995. "Revisiting Rokkan: On the Determinants of the Rise of Democracy in Europe." *Historical Social Research* 20(2): 161–87.

Ertman, Thomas. 1997. *Birth of the Leviathan: Building States and Regimes in Medieval and Early Modern Europe*. New York, NY: Cambridge University Press.

Estache, Antonio and Danny Leipziger, eds., 2009. *Fiscal Incidence and Middle Class: Implications for Policy*. Washington, DC: Brookings Institution Press.

Evans, Peter B. 1995. *Embedded Autonomy: States and Industrial Transformation*. Princeton, NJ: Princeton University Press.

Falleti, Tulia G. and James Mahoney. 2015. "The Comparative Sequential Method," in James Mahoney and Kathleen Thelen, eds., *Advances in Comparative-Historical Analysis*. New York, NY: Cambridge University Press, pp. 211–39.

Ferraro, Agustin E. 2011. "A Splendid Ruined Reform: The Creation and Destruction of a Civil Service in Argentina," in Andrew Massey, ed., *International Handbook on Civil Service Systems*. Cheltenham: Edward Elgar, pp. 152–17.

Finer, Herman. 1932. *The Theory and Practice of Modern Government*. Vol. 2. London: Methuen & Co.

Finer, S. E. 1962. *The Man on Horseback: The Role of the Military in Politics*. London: Pall Mall Press.

  1975. "State- and Nation-Building in Europe: The Role of the Military," in Charles Tilly, ed., *The Formation of National States in Western Europe*. Princeton, NJ: Princeton University Press, pp. 84–163.

  1997a. *The History of Government from the Earliest Times*. Vol. 1: *Ancient Monarchies and Empires*. New York, NY: Oxford University Press.

  1997b. *The History of Government from the Earliest Times*. Vol. 3: *Empires, Monarchies, and the Modern State*. New York, NY: Oxford University Press.

Flora, Peter, et al. 1983. *State, Economy, and Society in Western Europe 1815–1975*. Vol. 1. Frankfurt: Campus Verlag.

Foweraker, Joe. 2018 *Polity: Demystifying Democracy in Latin America and Beyond*. Boulder, CO: Lynne Rienner.

Friedrich, Carl J. 1950. *Constitutional Government and Democracy*. New York, NY: Ginn and Company.

Fukuyama, Francis. 2005. "'Stateness' First." *Journal of Democracy* 16(1): 84–88.

2011. *The Origins of Political Order: From Prehuman Times to the French Revolution.* New York, NY: Farrar, Straus and Giroux.

2014. *Political Order and Political Decay. From the Industrial Revolution to the Globalization of Democracy.* New York, NY: Farrar, Straus and Giroux.

Gandhi, Jennifer. 2008. *Political Institutions under Dictatorship.* New York, NY: Cambridge University Press.

Garrard, John. 2002. *Democratisation in Britain: Elites, Civil Society and Reform Since 1800.* New York, NY: Palgrave.

Garretón, Manuel Antonio. 2007. *Del post-pinochetismo a la sociedad democrática. Globalización y Política en el bicentenario.* Santiago, Chile: Debate.

Garretón, Manuel Antonio, Marcelo Cavarozzi, Peter S. Cleaves, Gary Gereffi, and Jonathan Hartlyn. 2004. *América Latina en el siglo XXI: Hacia una nueva matriz sociopolítica.* Santiago de Chile: LOM Ediciones.

Geddes, Barbara. 1994. *Politician's Dilemma: Building State Capacity in Latin America.* Berkeley, CA: University of California Press.

Gerlich, Peter. 1973. "The Institutionalization of European Parliaments," in Allan Kornberg, ed., *Legislatures in Comparative Perspective.* New York, NY: David McKay, pp. 94–113.

Germani, Gino. 1962. *Política y sociedad en una época de transición.* Buenos Aires: Editoial Paidós.

Gerschenkron, Alexander. 1943. *Bread and Democracy in Germany.* Berkeley, CA: University of California Press.

1962. *Economic Backwardness in Historical Perspective: A Book of Essays.* Cambridge, MA: Belknap Press of Harvard University Press.

1970. *Europe in the Russian Mirror: Four Lectures in Economic History.* New York, NY: Cambridge University Press.

Gibson, Edward L. 2012. *Boundary Control: Subnational Authoritarianism in Federal Democracies.* New York, NY: Cambridge University Press.

Giraudy, Agustina. 2015. *Democrats and Autocrats. Pathways of Subnational Undemocratic Regime Continuity within Democratic Countries.* New York, NY: Oxford University Press.

Giraudy, Agustina and Juan Pablo Luna. 2017. "Unpacking the State's Uneven Territorial Reach: Evidence from Latin America," in Miguel A. Centeno, Atul Kohli, and Deborah J. Yashar, eds., *States in the Developing World.* New York, NY: Cambridge University Press, pp. 93–120.

Glete, Jan. 2002. *War and the State in Early Modern Europe: Spain, the Dutch Republic and Sweden as Fiscal-Military States, 1500–1660.* New York, NY: Routledge.

Goldstein, Robert Justin. 1983. *Political Repression in 19th Century Europe.* London: Croom Helm.

Gomes, Ciro Ferreira and Roberto Mangabeira Unger. 1996. *O próximo passo: Uma alternativa prática ao neoliberalismo.* Rio de Janeiro: Topbooks.

González-Bustamante, Bastián. 2018. "Civil Service Models in Latin America," in Ali Farazmand, ed., *Global Encyclopedia of Public Administration, Public Policy, and Governance.* Cham, Switzerland: Springer International Publishing, pp. 775–83.

González-Bustamante, Bastián, Alejandro Olivares L., Pedro Abarca, and Esteban Molina. 2016. "Servicio civil en Chile, análisis de los directivos de primer nivel jerárquico (2003–13)." *Revista de Administração Pública* 50(1): 59–80.

Graham, Lawrence S. 1968. *Civil Service Reform in Brazil: Principles Versus Practice.* Austin, TX: University of Texas Press.

   1998. "The State in Retreat in the Administrative Field," in Menno Vellinga, ed., *The Changing Role of the State in Latin America.* New York, NY: Routledge, pp. 149–62.

Grew, Raymond, ed., 1978. *Crises of Political Development in Europe and the United States.* Princeton, NJ: Princeton University Press.

Grindle, Merilee S. 2012. *Jobs for the Boys: Patronage and the State in Comparative Perspective.* Cambridge, MA: Harvard University Press.

Gudynas, Eduardo. 2015. *Extractivismos. Ecología, economía y política de un modo de entender el desarrollo y la Naturaleza.* Cochabamba, Bolivia: Centro de Documentación e Información Bolivia/Centro Latino Americano de Ecología Social.

Haggard, Stephen and Robert Kaufman. 2016. *Dictators and Democrats: Elites, Masses, and Regime Change.* Princeton, NJ: Princeton University Press.

Hagopian, Frances. 1994. "Traditional Politics against State Transformation in Brazil," in Joel S. Migdal, Atul Kohli, and Vivienne Shue eds., *State Power and Social Forces: Domination and Transformation.* New York, NY: Cambridge University Press, pp. 37–64.

   1996. *Traditional Politics and Regime Change in Brazil.* New York, NY: Cambridge University Press.

He, Baogang. 2001. "The National Identity Problem and Democratization: Rustow's Theory of Sequence." *Government and Opposition* 36(1): 97–119.

Heine, Jorge and Brigitte Weiffen. 2015. *21st Century Democracy Promotion in the Americas.* New York, NY: Routledge.

Hernández López, Mario Humberto. 2012. "Gobernanza corporativa y matriz institucional en México." *Gestión y Estrategia* 42: 17–34.

Hilgers, Tina and Laura Macdonald, eds., 2017. *Violence in Latin America and the Caribbean: Subnational Structures, Institutions, and Clientelist Networks*. New York, NY: Cambridge University Press.

Hintze, Otto. 1975a [1902]. "The Formation of States and Constitutional Development: A Study in History and Politics," in Felix Gilbert, ed., *The Historical Essays of Otto Hintze*. New York, NY: Oxford University Press, pp. 157–77.

1975b [1906]. "Military Organization and the Organization of the State," in Felix Gilbert, ed., *The Historical Essays of Otto Hintze*. New York, NY: Oxford University Press, pp.180–215.

1975c [1931]. "The Preconditions of Representative Government in the Context of World History," in Felix Gilbert, ed., *The Historical Essays of Otto Hintze*. New York, NY: Oxford University Press, pp. 305–53.

Hirschman, Albert O. 1958. *The Strategy of Economic Development*. New Haven, CT: Yale University Press.

1963. *Journeys Toward Progress: Studies of Economic Policy-Making in Latin America*. New York, NY: Twentieth Century Fund.

1968. "The Political Economy of Import-Substituting Industrialization in Latin America." *Quarterly Journal of Economics* 82(1): 1–32.

1990. "The Case Against 'One Thing at a Time'." *World Development* 18(8): 1119–22.

Hoffman, Philip T. 1994. "Early Modern France, 1450–1700," in Philip T. Hoffman and Kathryn Norberg, eds., *Fiscal Crises, Liberty, and Representative Government, 1450–1789*. Stanford, CA: Stanford University Press, pp. 226–52.

Huber, Evelyne. 1995. "Assessments of State Strength," in Peter H. Smith, ed., *Latin America in Comparative Perspective: New Approaches to Methods and Analysis*. Boulder, CO: Westview Press, pp. 163–93.

Huber, Evelyne and John D. Stephens. 1999. "The Bourgeoisie and Democracy: Historical and Comparative Perspectives." *Social Research* 66(3): 759–88.

Hunter, Wendy and David S. Brown. 2000. "World Bank Directives, Domestic Interests, and the Politics of Human Capital Investment in Latin America." *Comparative Political Studies* 33(1): 113–43.

Huntington, Samuel P. 1968. *Political Order in Changing Societies*. New Haven, CT: Yale University Press.

Iacoviello, Mercedes. 2006. "Analysis comparativo por subsistemas," in Koldo Echebarría, ed., *Informe sobre la situación del servicio civil en América Latina*. Washington, DC: Inter-American Development Bank, pp. 533–72.

Iacoviello, Mercedes and Luciano Strazza. 2014. "Diagnóstico del servicio civil en América Latina," in Juan Carlos Cortázar, Mariano Lafuente, and Mario Sanginés, eds., *Al servicio del ciudadano: una década de reformas del servicio civil en América Latina (2004–13)*. Washington, DC: Inter-American Development Bank, pp. 13–58.

Kaufman, Robert R., and Joan Nelson. 2004. "Conclusions: The Political Dynamics of Reform," in Robert R. Kaufman and Joan Nelson, eds., *Crucial Needs, Weak Incentives*. Washington, DC and Baltimore, MD: Woodrow Wilson Center Press, and the Johns Hopkins University Press, pp. 473–519.

King, Desmond and Robert C. Lieberman. 2009. "Ironies of State Building: A Comparative Perspective on the American State." *World Politics* 61(3): 547–88.

Kingstone, Peter and Timothy J. Power, eds., 2017. *Democratic Brazil Divided*. Pittsburgh, PA: University of Pittsburgh Press.

Kitschelt, Herbert and Steven Wilkinson, eds., 2007. *Patrons, Clients and Policies: Patterns of Democratic Accountability and Political Competition*. New York, NY: Cambridge University Press.

Krasner, Stephen D. 1984. "Approaches to the State: Alternative Conceptions and Historical Dynamics." *Comparative Politics* 16(2): 223–46.

Kurth, James R. 1979. "Industrial Change and Political Change: A European Perspective," in David Collier, ed., *The New Authoritarianism in Latin America*. Princeton, NJ: Princeton University Press, pp. 319–62.

Kurtz, Marcus J. 2013. *Latin American State Building in Comparative Perspective: Social Foundations of Institutional Order*. New York, NY: Cambridge University Press.

Laitin, David D. 1995. "Transitions to Democracy and Territorial Integrity," in Adam Przeworski et al., eds., *Sustainable Democracy*. New York, NY: Cambridge University Press, pp. 19–33.

Lessing, Benjamin. 2017. *Making Peace in Drug Wars: Crackdowns and Cartels in Latin America*. New York, NY: Cambridge University Press.

Levi, Margaret. 1999. "Death and Taxes: Extractive Equality and the Development of Democratic Institutions," in Ian Shapiro and Casiano Hacker-Cordon, eds., *Democracy's Value*. New York, NY: Cambridge University Press, pp. 112–31.

Levitsky, Steven and Lucan A. Way. 2010. *Competitive Authoritarianism: Hybrid Regimes After the Cold War*. New York, NY: Cambridge University Press.

Linz, Juan J. and Alfred Stepan. 1996a. *Problems of Democratic Transition and Consolidation: Southern Europe, South America and Post-Communist Europe*. Baltimore, MD: The Johns Hopkins University Press.

1996b. "Toward Consolidated Democracies." *Journal of Democracy* 7(2): 14–33.

Llanos, Mariana and Leiv Mainstentredet, eds., 2010. *Presidential Breakdowns in Latin America, Causes and Outcomes of Executive Instability in Developing Democracies*. New York, NY: Palgrave.

Longo, Francisco. 2006. "Analysis comparativo por índices," in Koldo Echebarría, ed., *Informe sobre la situación del servicio civil en América Latina*. Washington, DC: Inter-American Development Bank, pp. 573–92.

Longo, Francisco and Carles Ramió, eds., 2008. *La profesionalización del empleo público en América Latina*. Barcelona: Fundació CIDOB.

López-Alves, Fernando. 2000. *State Formation and Democracy in Latin America, 1810–1900*. Durham, NC: Duke University Press.

Lora, Eduardo, ed., 2007. *El estado de las reformas del Estado en América Latina*. Washington, DC, and Bogotá : The Inter-American Development Bank, and Mayol.

Loveman, Brian. 1999. *For La Patria: Politics and the Armed Forces in Latin America*. Wilmington, DE: Scholarly Resources.

Luna, Juan Pablo. 2014. *Segmented Representation: Political Party Strategies in Unequal Democracies*. New York, NY: Oxford University Press.

Luna, Juan Pablo and Gerardo L. Munck. 2022 (forthcoming). *Introduction to Contemporary Latin American Politics: The Quest for Democracy and Citizenship Rights*. New York, NY: Cambridge University Press.

Mainwaring, Scott and Aníbal Pérez-Liñán. 2014. *Democracies and Dictatorships in Latin America. Emergence, Survival, and Fall*. New York, NY: Cambridge University Press.

Mann, Michael. 1986. *The Sources of Social Power*. Vol. 1. *A History of Power from the Beginning to A.D. 1760*. Cambridge: Cambridge University Press.

1993. *The Sources of Social Power*. Vol. 2: *The Rise of Classes and Nation-States, 1760–1914*. Cambridge: Cambridge University Press.

2008. "Infrastructural Power Revisited." *Studies in Comparative International Development* 43(3): 355–65.

Mansfield, Edward D. and Jack L. Snyder. 2007. "The Sequencing 'Fallacy'." *Journal of Democracy* 18(3): 5–10.

Manzetti, Luigi and Charles H. Blake. 1996. "Market Reforms and Corruption in Latin America: New Means for Old Ways." *Review of International Political Economy* 3(4): 662–97.

Markoff, John. 1996. *The Abolition of Feudalism: Peasants, Lords, and Legislation in the French Revolution*. Philadelphia, PA: University of Pennsylvania Press.

Marshall, T. H. 1950. "Citizenship and Social Class," in T.H. Marshall, ed., *Citizenship and Social Class, and Other Essays*. Cambridge: Cambridge University Press, pp. 1–85.

Mazzuca, Sebastián L. 2010. "Access to Power Versus Exercise of Power: Reconceptualizing the Quality of Democracy in Latin America." *Studies in Comparative International Development* 45(3): 334–57.

2013. "The Rise of Rentier Populism." *Journal of Democracy* 24(2): 108–22.

2021. *Latecomer State Formation. Political Geography and Capacity Failure in Latin America*. New Haven, CT: Yale University Press.

Mazzuca, Sebastián L. and Gerardo L. Munck. 2014. "State or Democracy First? Alternative Perspectives on the State-Democracy Nexus." *Democratization* 21(7): 1221–43.

Mazzuca, Sebastián L. and James A. Robinson. 2009. "Political Conflict and Power Sharing in the Origins of Modern Colombia." *Hispanic American Historical Review* 89(2): 285–321.

Mears, John A. 1969. "The Emergence of the Standing Professional Army in Seventeenth-Century Europe." *Social Science Quarterly* 50(1): 106–15.

Meltzer, Allan H. and Scott F. Richard. 1981. "A Rational Theory of the Size of Government." *Journal of Political Economy* 89(5): 914–27.

Mickey, Robert. 2015. *Paths Out of Dixie: The Democratization of Authoritarian Enclaves in America's Deep South, 1944–1972*. Princeton, NJ: Princeton University Press.

Møller, Jørgen. 2015. "The Medieval Roots of Democracy." *Journal of Democracy* 26(3): 110–23.

Møller, Jørgen and Svend-Erik Skaaning. 2011. "Stateness First?" *Democratization* 18(1): 1–24.

Moore, Jr., Barrington. 1966. *Social Origins of Dictatorship and Democracy. Lord and Peasant in the Making of the Modern World*. Boston, MA: Beacon Press.

Morlino, Leonardo. 2011. *Changes for Democracy. Actors, Structures, Processes*. Oxford: Oxford University Press.

Morris, Stephen D. 2009. *Political Corruption in Mexico. The Impact of Democratization*. Boulder, CO: Lynne Rienner Publishers.

Munck, Gerardo L. 2015. "Building Democracy … Which Democracy? Ideology and Models of Democracy in Post-Transition Latin America." *Government and Opposition* 50(3): 364–93.

2016. "What is Democracy? A Reconceptualization of the Quality of Democracy." *Democratization* 23(1): 1–26.

Nettl, J. P. 1968. "The State as a Conceptual Variable." *World Politics* 20(4): 559–92.

Nichter, Simeon. 2018. *Votes for Survival: Relational Clientelism in Latin America*. New York, NY: Cambridge University Press,

Nordlinger, Eric A. 1968. "Political Development: Time Sequences and Rates of Change." *World Politics* 20(3): 494–520.

Norris, Pippa. 2012. *Making Democratic Governance Work*. New York, NY: Cambridge University Press.

North, Douglass C., John Joseph Wallis, and Barry R. Weingast. 2009. *Violence and Social Orders: A Conceptual Framework for Interpreting Recorded Human History*. New York, NY: Cambridge University Press.

North, Liisa, Blanca Rubio, and Alberto Acosta, eds., 2020. *Concentración económica y poder político en América Latina*. Mexico: Fundación Friedrich Ebert and Clacso.

Nunberg, Barbara and Regina Silvia Pacheco. 2016. "Public Management Incongruity in 21st Century Brazil," in Ben Ross Schneider, ed., *New Order and Progress: Development and Democracy in Brazil*. New York, NY: Oxford University Press, pp. 134–61.

OAS (Organization of American States). 2011. *Política, dinero y poder. Un dilema para las democracias de las Américas*. Mexico: OAS and Fondo de Cultura Económica.

O'Donnell, Guillermo. 1972. *Modernización y autoritarismo*. Buenos Aires: Editorial Paidós.

1981. "Las fuerzas armadas y el estado autoritario del cono sur de América Latina," in Norbert Lechner, ed., *Estado y política en America Latina*. Mexico: Siglo XXI, pp. 199–235.

1993. "On the State, Democratization and Some Conceptual Problems (A Latin American View with Glances at Some Post-Communist Countries)." *World Development* 21(8): 1355–70.

1998. "Poverty and Inequality in Latin America: Some Political Reflections," in Víctor Tokman and Guillermo O'Donnell, eds., *Poverty and Inequality in Latin America. Issues and New Challenges*. South Bend, IN.: University of Notre Dame Press, pp. 49–71.

2001. "Democracy, Law, and Comparative Politics." *Studies in Comparative International Development* 36(1): 7–36.

2010. *Democracia, agencia y Estado: Teoría con intención comparativa*. Buenos Aires: Prometeo Libros.

Panizza, Francisco, Conrado Ricardo Ramos Larraburu, and Gerardo Scherlis. 2018. "Unpacking Patronage: The Politics of Patronage Appointments in Argentina's and Uruguay's Central Public Administrations." *Journal of Politics in Latin America* 10(3): 59–98.

Paramio, Ludolfo, ed., 2010. *Clases medias y gobernabilidad en América Latina*. Madrid: Editorial Pablo Iglesias.

Paredes, Maritza. 2013. *Shaping State Capacity: A Comparative Historical Analysis of Mining Dependence in the Andes, 1840s–1920s*. PhD Dissertation, University of Oxford. https://ethos.bl.uk/OrderDetails.do?uin=uk.bl.ethos.600803

Penfold, Michael and Guillermo Rodríguez Guzmán. 2014. "The Growing but Vulnerable Middle Class in Latin America. Growth Patterns, Values and Preferences." *Public Policy and Productive Transformation Series* No 17. Caracas: Corporación Andina de Fomento.

Perina, Rubén M. 2015. *The Organization of American States as the Advocate and Guardian of Democracy*. Lanham, MD: University Press of America.

Polanyi, Karl. 1944. *The Great Transformation: The Political and Economic Origins of Our Time*. Boston, MA: Beacon Press.

Portes, Alejandro and Kelly Hoffman. 2003. "Latin American Class Structures: Their Composition and Change during the Neoliberal Era." *Latin American Research Review* 38(1): 41–82.

Przeworski, Adam. 1975. "Institutionalization of Voting Patterns, or is Mobilization the Source of Decay?" *American Political Science Review* 69(1): 49–67.

2010. *Democracy and the Limits of Self-Government*. New York, NY: Cambridge University Press.

2015. "Political Institutions and Political Order(s)," in Adam Przeworski, ed., *Democracy in a Russian Mirror*. New York, NY: Cambridge University Press, pp. 247–67.

2019. *Crises of Democracy*. New York, NY: Cambridge University Press.

Przeworski, Adam, Tamar Asadurian, and Anjali Thomas Bohlken. 2012. "The Origins of Parliamentary Responsibility," in Tom Ginsburg, ed., *Comparative Constitutional Design*. New York, NY: Cambridge University Press, pp. 101–37.

Raadschelders Jos C. N. and Marie-Louise Bemelmans-Videc. 2015. "Political (System) Reform: Can Administrative Reform Succeed Without?" in Frits M. van der Meer, Jos C. N. Raadschelders, and Theo A. J. Toonen, eds., *Comparative Civil Service Systems in the 21st Century*, 2nd ed. New York, NY: Palgrave Macmillan, pp. 334–53.

Remmer, Karen. 1991. *Military Rule in Latin America*. Boulder, CO: Westview Press.

Rettberg, Angelika. 2005. "Business versus Business? *Grupos* and Organized Business in Colombia." *Latin American Politics and Society* 47(1): 31–54.

Richards, Peter G. 1963. *Patronage in British Government*. London: Allen and Unwin.

Riggs, Fred W. 1963. "Bureaucracy and Political Development: A Paradoxical View," in Joseph LaPalombara, ed., *Bureaucracy and Political Development*. Princeton, NJ: Princeton University Press, pp. 120–67.

Ringen, Stein. 2007. *What Democracy is For: On Freedom and Moral Government*. Princeton, NJ: Princeton University Press.

Rokkan, Stein. 1970. *Citizens, Elections, and Parties: Approaches to the Comparative Study of the Processes of Development*. New York, NY: David McKay.

1975. "Dimensions of State Formation and Nation-Building: A Possible Paradigm for Research on Variation within Europe," in Charles Tilly, ed., *The Formation of National States in Western Europe*. Princeton, NJ: Princeton University Press, pp. 562–600.

Rose, Richard and Doh Chull Shin. 2001. "Democratization Backwards: The Problem of Third-Wave Democracies." *British Journal of Political Science* 31(2): 331–54.

Rosenberg, Hans. 1958. *Bureaucracy, Aristocracy, and Autocracy: The Prussian Experience, 1660–1815*. Cambridge, MA: Harvard University Press.

Rosenfeld, Bryn. 2017. "Reevaluating the Middle-Class Protest Paradigm: A Case-Control Study of Democratic Protest Coalitions in Russia." *American Political Science Review* 111(4): 637–52.

Rouquié, Alain. 1987. *The Military and the State in Latin America*. Berkeley, CA: University of California Press.

Rueschemeyer, Dietrich, Evelyne Huber Stephens, and John D. Stephens. 1992. *Capitalist Development and Democracy*. Chicago, IL: University of Chicago Press.

Rustow, Dankwart A. 1967. *A World of Nations: Problems of Political Modernization*. Washington, DC: Brookings Institution.

1970. "Transitions to Democracy: Toward a Dynamic Model." *Comparative Politics* 2(3): 337–63.

Saunders, Robert. 2011. *Democracy and the Vote in British Politics, 1848–1867: The Making of the Second Reform Act*. Farnham: Ashgate.

Saylor, Ryan. 2014. *State Building in Boom Times: Commodities and Coalitions in Latin America and Africa*. Oxford: Oxford University Press.

Schmitter, Philippe and Terry Karl. 1991. "What Democracy is . . . and What it is Not." *Journal of Democracy* 2(3): 75–88.

Schneider, Aaron. 2012. *State-Building and Tax Regimes in Central America*. New York, NY: Cambridge University Press.

Schneider, Ben Ross. 2004. *Business Politics and the State in Twentieth-Century Latin America*. New York, NY: Cambridge University Press.

2013. *Hierarchical Capitalism in Latin America: Business, Labor, and the Challenges of Equitable Development*. New York, NY: Cambridge University Press.

Shefter, Martin. 1994. *Political Parties and the State: The American Historical Experience*. Princeton, NJ: Princeton University Press.

Silberman, Bernard S. 1993. *Cages of Reason: The Rise of the Rational State in France, Japan, the United States, and Great Britain*. Chicago, IL: University of Chicago Press.

Skocpol, Theda. 1979. *States and Social Revolutions: A Comparative Analysis of France, Russia, and China*. New York, NY: Cambridge University Press.

Skowronek, Stephen. 1982. *Building a New American State: The Expansion of National Administrative Capacities, 1877–1920*. New York, NY: Cambridge University Press.

Slater, Dan. 2008. "Can Leviathan be Democratic? Competitive Elections, Robust Mass Politics, and State Infrastructural Power." *Studies in Comparative International Development* 43(3): 252–72.

Smith, Peter and Cameron Sells. 2017. *Democracy in Latin America*, 3rd ed. New York, NY: Oxford University Press.

Snyder, Jack. 2000. *From Voting to Violence: Democratization and Nationalist Conflict*. New York, NY: Norton.

Soifer, Hillel David. 2015. *State-Building in Latin America*. New York, NY: Cambridge University Press.

Stillman, Richard. J. 2015. "Is Past Prologue to 21st-Century Civil Service Systems? Exploring Historical Frames for Discovering Lessons about Institutional Futures," in Frits M. van der Meer, Jos C. N. Raadschelders, and Theo A. J. Toonen, eds., *Comparative Civil Service Systems in the 21st Century*, 2nd ed. New York, NY: Palgrave Macmillan, pp. 301–16.

Stokes, Susan C., Thad Dunning, Marcelo Nazareno, and Valeria Brusco. 2013. *Brokers, Voters, and Clientelism: The Puzzle of Distributive Politics*. New York, NY: Cambridge University Press.

Stone, Randall W. 2008. "The Scope of IMF Conditionality." *International Organization* 62(4): 589–620.

Svampa, Maristella. 2019. *Las fronteras del neoextractivismo en América Latina: Conflictos socioambientales, giro ecoterritorial y nuevas dependencias*. Bielefeld, Germany: Verlag.

Taylor, Matthew M. 2019. "The Troubling Strength of Brazilian Institutions in the Face of Scandal." *Taiwan Journal of Democracy* 15(1): 91–111.

Thelen, Kathleen. 1999. "Historical Institutionalism in Comparative Politics." *Annual Review of Political Science* 2: 369–404.

Tilly, Charles. 1989. "State and Counterrevolution in France." *Social Research* 56(1): 71–97.

1990. *Coercion, Capital, and European States, AD 990–1990*. Oxford: Basil Blackwell.

1993. *European Revolutions, 1492–1992*. Oxford: Basil Blackwell.

1998. "Where Do Rights Come From?" in Theda Skocpol, ed., *Democracy, Revolution, and History*. Ithaca, NY: Cornell University Press, pp. 55–72.

2004. *Contention and Democracy in Europe, 1650–2000*. New York, NY: Cambridge University Press.

2006. *Regimes and Repertoires*. Chicago, IL: University of Chicago Press.

2007. *Democracy*. New York, NY: Cambridge University Press.

Tocqueville, Alexis de. 2010 [1835 and 1840]. *Democracy in America* 4 Vols. Indianapolis, IN: Liberty Fund.

2011 [1856]. *The Ancien Régime and the French Revolution*. New York, NY: Cambridge University Press.

Touraine, Alain. 1989. *América Latina. Política y sociedad*. Madrid: Espasa-Calpe.

Unger, Roberto Mangabeira. 1987. *False Necessity: Anti-Necessitarian Social Theory in the Service of Radical Democracy*. New York, NY: Cambridge University Press.

1990. *A Alternativa Transformadora. Como Democratizar o Brasil*. Rio de Janeiro: Editora Guanabara Koogan.

UNODC. 2019. *Global Study on Homicide 2019*. Vienna, Austria: UNODC.

Valenzuela, Arturo. 2004. "Latin American Presidencies Interrupted." *Journal of Democracy* 15(4): 5–19.

von Beyme, Klaus. 2000. *Parliamentary Democracy: Democratization, Destabilization, Reconsolidation, 1789–1999*. New York, NY: St. Martin's Press.

Vu, Tuong. 2020. "State-Building and Democratization: The Sequencing Debate and Evidence from East Asia," in Aurel Croissant and Olli Hellmann, eds., *Stateness and Democracy in East Asia*. New York, NY: Cambridge University Press, pp. 25–46.

Waldner, David. 2015. "What Makes Process Tracing Good: Causal Mechanisms, Causal Inference, and the Completeness Standard in Comparative Politics," in Andrew Bennett and Jeffrey T. Checkel, eds., *Process Tracing: From Metaphor to Analytic Tool*. New York, NY: Cambridge University Press, pp. 126–52.

Weber, Max. 1946 [1919]. "Politics as a Vocation," in H.H. Gerth and C. Wright Mills, eds., *From Max Weber: Essays in Sociology*. New York, NY: Oxford University Press, pp. 77–128.

1978 [1922]. *Economy and Society*. Berkeley, CA: University of California Press.

1994a [1905]. "On the Situation of Constitutional Democracy in Russia," in Max Weber, *Weber: Political Writings*. Cambridge: Cambridge University Press, pp. 29–74.

1994b [1917]. "Suffrage and Democracy in Germany," in Max Weber, ed., *Weber: Political Writings*. Cambridge: Cambridge University Press, pp. 80–129.

Weiner, Myron. 1971. "Political Participation: Crisis of the Political Process," in Leonard Binder, James Smoot Coleman, Joseph LaPalombara, Lucian Pye, Sidney Verba, and Myron Weiner, eds., *Crises and Sequences in Political Development*. Princeton, NJ: Princeton University Press, pp. 159–204.

Weingast, Barry R. 1998. "Political Stability and Civil War: Institutions, Commitment, and American Democracy," in Robert H. Bates et al., eds., *Analytic Narratives*. Princeton, NJ: Princeton University Press, pp. 148–93.

Wilson, Peter. 1999. "Warfare in the Old Regime 1648–1789," in Jeremy Black, ed., *European Warfare 1453–1815*. New York, NY: St. Martin's Press, pp. 69–95.

Wimmer, Andreas. 2013. *Waves of War. Nationalism, State-Formation, and Ethnic Exclusion in the Modern World*. New York, NY: Cambridge University Press.

Wimmer, Andreas and Conrad Schetter. 2003. "Putting State-Formation First: Some Recommendations for Reconstruction and Peace-Making in Afghanistan." *Journal of International Development* 15(5): 525–39.

Wise, Carol. 2020. *Dragonomics: How Latin America is Maximizing (or Missing Out on) China's International Development Strategy*. New Haven, CT: Yale University Press.

Wood, Gordon S. 1969. *The Creation of the American Republic, 1776–1787*. Chapel Hill, NC: University of North Carolina Press.

World Bank. 2017. *World Development Report 2017. Governance and the Law*. Washington, DC: The World Bank.

Yashar, Deborah J. 2018. *Homicidal Ecologies: Illicit Economies and Complicit States in Latin America*. New York, NY: Cambridge University Press.

Zakaria, Fareed. 2003. *The Future of Freedom: Illiberal Democracy at Home and Abroad*. New York, NY: W. W. Norton.

Ziblatt, Daniel. 2017. *Conservative Parties and the Birth of Democracy*. New York, NY: Cambridge University Press.

Acknowledgments

We would like to acknowledge the useful comments from Kent Eaton, Tulia Falleti, Agustina Giraudy, Lucas González, Juan Pablo Luna, Victoria Murillo, Maria Paula Saffon, Andrew Schrank, and four anonymous reviewers.

Cambridge Elements ≡

Elements in Politics and Society in Latin America

Maria Victoria Murillo

Columbia University

Maria Victoria Murillo is Professor of Political Science and International Affairs at Columbia University. She is the author of *Political Competition, Partisanship, and Policymaking in the Reform of Latin American Public Utilities* (Cambridge, 2009). She is also editor of *Carreras Magisteriales, Desempeño Educativo y Sindicatos de Maestros en América Latina* (2003), and co-editor of *Argentine Democracy: the Politics of Institutional Weakness* (2005). She has published in edited volumes as well as in the *American Journal of Political Science, World Politics, Comparative Political Studies* among others.

Juan Pablo Luna

The Pontifical Catholic University of Chile

Juan Pablo Luna is Professor in the Department of Political Science at The Pontifical Catholic University of Chile. He is the author of *Segmented Representation. Political Party Strategies in Unequal Democracies*, and has co-authored *Latin American Party Systems* (Cambridge, 2010). His work on political representation, state capacity, and organized crime has appeared in *Comparative Political Studies, Revista de Ciencia Política*, the *Journal of Latin American Studies, Latin American Politics and Society, Studies in Comparative International Development* among others.

Tulia G. Falleti

University of Pennsylvania

Tulia G. Falleti is the Class of 1965 Term Associate Professor of Political Science, Director of the Latin American and Latino Studies Program, and Senior Fellow of the Leonard Davis Institute for Health Economics at the University of Pennsylvania. She is the author of the award-winning *Decentralization and Subnational Politics in Latin America* (Cambridge, 2010). She is co-editor of *The Oxford Handbook of Historical Institutionalism*, among other edited books. Her articles have appeared in many edited volumes and journals such as the *American Political Science Review* and *Comparative Political Studies*.

Andrew Schrank

Brown University

Andrew Schrank is the Olive C. Watson Professor of Sociology and International & Public Affairs at Brown University. His articles on business, labor, and the state in Latin America have appeared in the *American Journal of Sociology, Comparative Politics, Comparative Political Studies, Latin American Politics & Society, Social Forces*, and *World Development*, among other journals, and his co-authored book, *Root-Cause Regulation: Labor Inspection in Europe and the Americas*, is out soon.

About the Series

Latin American politics and society are at a crossroads, simultaneously confronting serious challenges and remarkable opportunities that are likely to be shaped by formal institutions and informal practices alike. The new Politics and Society in Latin America Cambridge Elements series will offer multidisciplinary and methodologically pluralist contributions on the most important topics and problems confronted by the region.

Printed in the United States
By Bookmasters